# Endorsements

## OF CLAY CLARK

"Clay, you've become an influencer. More than anything else, you have evolved into an influencer where your word has more and more power. As you know, there is alot of fake influencers out there. I'm glad that you and I agree so much. You are on it man! Everybody listen to this guy. He knows what he's talking about."

**- Robert Kiyosaki**

*(The best-selling author of The Rich Dad Poor Dad book series and a man who has sold over 40 million copies of his entrepreneur books.)*

"Clay Clark is an entrepreneur extraordinaire."

**- David Robinson**

*(NBA Hall of Basketball Player, former NBA MVP, NBA Championship Winner & Investor.)*

"He's like Steve Martin meets Steve Forbes."

**- Jim Stovall**

*(New York Times best-selling self-help writer best known for his bestselling novel The Ultimate Gift. The book was made into the movie The Ultimate Gift, distributed by 20th Century Fox. The Ultimate Gift has a prequel called The Ultimate Life and a sequel called The Ultimate Legacy.)*

"For the last two years, I have come to Clay Clark's *Thrivetime Show* conference/seminar, and I must say I didn't know what to expect at first, but it's EXCEPTIONAL. If you are serious, and I mean really serious about your career, your entrepreneurship, and your wealth creation ability. I strongly, implore you to come to Tulsa, invest the two days, it will change your life. It's quite extraordinary, and I'm a tough grader."

**- Michael Levine**

*(The publicist and public relations expert of choice for 58 Academy Award winners, 34 Grammy Award winners, and 43 New York Times best-sellers including Michael Jackson, Barbra Streisand, Prince, Nike, and others.)*

**PAWS**, for a
Notable Quotable

"The difference between great people and everyone else is that great people create their lives actively, while everyone else is created by their lives, passively waiting to see where life takes them next. The difference between the two is living fully and just existing."

**-MICHAEL GERBER**

*(Best-selling author of The E-Myth Revisited)*

FEATURING CELEBRITY DOG, "ACHILLES"

# Make Your Dog Epic

## Building an Epic Bond:
### Understanding Your Dog's Training Journey

# J.T. LAWSON & CLAY CLARK

(Author of *What I Learned from my Millionaire Mentor*. Real estate investor, lead trainer and owner of Make Your Dog Epic Oklahoma location.)

(Former U.S. SBA Young Entrepreneur of the Year, the 6x iTunes chart-topping podcast host of the ThrivetimeShow, and *Forbes* Coaches Council member, Clay Clark.)

We provide website, answer initial calls, and branding, as well as offer other support you can access at will.

# Happy Paw·lidays

## Behold, An Epic, Mind-Expanding, Dog Training Festival Of Literary Wonder!

**Make Your Dog Epic**
Building an Epic Bond

ISBN: 979-8-9908526-1-7

Copyright © by Clay Clark

**Clay Clark Publishing**
Published by Clay Clark Publishing
3920 West 91st Street South
Tulsa, OK 74132

# Table of Contents

**PAWS**, for a
Notable Quotable

# "A goal is a dream with a deadline."

### -NAPOLEON HILL
*(The best-selling author of Think & Grow Rich.)*

# Introduction

## ABOUT THE CO-FOUNDER, PETER TAUNTON

The Make Your Dog Epic dog training franchise experience was created by the founder of Snap Fitness (which has over 2,500 locations in 26 countries), Peter Taunton and Oklahoma's U.S. SBA Young Entrepreneur of the Year Clay Clark. With a multi-decade history of success, Peter Taunton and Clay Clark designed the franchise systems so that you, as a Make Your Dog Epic dog training franchise owner, can spend nearly all of your time training dogs and training your incredible staff how to train dogs while our laser-focused franchise support team manages the repetitive and often tedious marketing, scheduling center, search engine optimization, customer relationship management software, and most aspects of the money collection side of the business for you.

Peter Taunton is a pioneer in the fitness industry. In 2003, he had a vision for Snap Fitness: to create an affordable, 24-7, results-driven gym differentiated from the impersonal, expensive big-box experience. Today, there are Snap Fitness franchises in 2,500 locations in 26 countries. Peter created the Peter Taunton Foundation that supports families of fallen soldiers and also stands against poaching. For Taunton, it comes down to one word: passion. He has it, he teaches it, and the results speak for themselves. Even as his operations expand, he remains ever-committed to providing owners and members with the tools and programs they need to reach life-changing goals.

Peter grew up one of seven children in a small midwestern town in Willmar, Minnesota. He grew up from humble beginnings attending a two-room schoolhouse. After finishing high school Peter paid his own way through the first three years of college at St. Cloud State University in Minnesota. But by junior year he recalls sitting in a business statistics class, feeling frustrated by the subject matter, burdened by accumulating tuition debt and tired of living paycheck to paycheck. At breakfast one morning with his twin brother Paul, Peter had enough and promptly closed his textbook announcing that he was quitting college. His brother would go on to quit that same day. Keeping the decision secret from their parents, the brothers would finish out the semester living in their dorm room and honing in on their racquetball skills.

Peter had first picked up a racquet at age thirteen and still remembers how natural he adapted to the sport. With a tremendous amount of practice, his level increased dramatically, eventually becoming a sponsored player for Ektelon and turning pro. The discipline and dedication learned while playing at such a high level would later fuel his success in business. His discipline, consistency, and competitive nature, found him and his brother ranked as the No. 2 doubles team in the country.

Read Peter Taunton's Book Impossible Hill Today:

**IMPOSSIBLE HILL**
Everyone has an Impossible Hill. Anyone can become a Hilltaker. Are you ready to take the Impossible Hill of your dreams? If you've ever desired to create your own business or you've started your journey as an entrepreneur and especially if you've created momentum building a company.

# Introduction

**A NOTE FROM CO-FOUNDER, CLAY CLARK**

I want to give this short book to all of our wonderful clients, locations, and hard-working owners because I believe it's important to be extremely transparent about how we train dogs and my proven philosophy of how we run our business.

Whether you're a client seeking our expertise, a dedicated Make Your Dog Epic employee in training, a committed Make Your Dog Epic owner, or simply an eager learner looking to dive into the world of dog training, know this: Our unwavering mission revolves around one singular goal-creating, well-behaved, joyful dogs alongside their equally joyful owners. No one dog is the same, and no one owner is the same. This is why we offer our first lesson for 50 cents. We want to figure out what it will take to get each dog to their owner's goals. The question I thought about throughout the process of creating this system is:

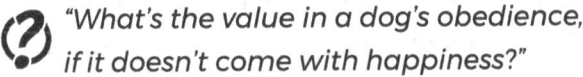

*"What's the value in a dog's obedience,*
*if it doesn't come with happiness?"*

Our goal is: "Obedience but NEVER at the expense of personality." There are many ways to train a dog and there is no regulatory body over dog training in the United States. It would be the equivalent of being a doctor, but not needing to go to school, or aspiring to be like a lawyer, but the Bar Exam being voluntary.

Then, even if you did take the Bar Exam, there is no governing body over it making sure they are meeting certain standards.

Basically, when it comes to dog training certifications and experience, doesn't mean anything. Because there is no governing body over certifications, they could've been doing it wrong for the last 20 years. Just because you have experience in something doesn't mean it's good experience. What matters is happy customers. We pride ourselves on having the happiest clients who leave raving reviews and testimonials about us. That's all that matters. As a trainer or licensee with Make Your Dog Epic, our #1 goal is happy dogs and happy clients!

In this short training guide, I teach our training standards and the workflow we actually use to run our business.

## WHAT DOES CLAY CLARK DO?

Clay Clark helps clients and himself to scale and grow successful, sustainable and profitable businesses. See thousands of documented Clay Clark client success stories today at: https://www.thrivetimeshow.com/testimonials/

"Clay Clark has been recognized nationally by the White House as Oklahoma's Small Business Entrepreneur of the Year, and he still hasn't reached the sea-soned age of forty. He has learned to leverage his business acumen and now finds himself in multiple successful business partnerships.So I was not surprised at all when he set out to launch Thrive15.com – the place to get what you need to know to get you where you want to go. Those are his words. This book extends his winning talks beyond sold-out conferences to an audience of thousands morenation wide and around the world. And through Thrive15.com, he will open up passageways for others to live beyond the "just surviving" mentality. He celebrates success wherever it is found. He understands the hard work and dedication required. He really does admire Napoleon Hill and fills his life with Mr. Hill's actionable quotes. They are all through this book. As I look at Clay's success and his larger-than-life vision for his future, he is well on his way to emulating the man he so admires. And quite frankly, he is placing him in a similar position to be admired and quoted as his life and businesses continue to THRIVE. Oftentimes people offering advice simply trust that the mes-sage is understood and move on, but not Clay Clark. He is committed to being in your face for your success. Not afraid of repetitious conversation and in-your-face humor, he is committed to each reader getting the message and more importantly, implementing the action steps set forth in this book and those voiced at Thrive15.com.Embracing and implementing the action steps in his books and training. Clay Clark is obsessed with implementing the action steps around your "big idea." This man gets emotional over your business success – maximizing your talents and potential. He remembers his dorm-room start and fully celebrates yours. Quoting Clay, "My friend, as you can tell by now, running a successful business is about so much more than just having a 'big idea.'

Your BIG IDEA is important, but the overwhelming majority of what will make your business succeed or fail has little to do with the 'big idea itself and everything to do with the execution of the 'big idea.'" Clay Leaves us no doubt that action on our part matters. His life as well as his insightful consulting encounters become a clear window through which we can look and see what is possible in many of our lives if we are willing to put in the time and effort necessary to turn ideas into reality. Clay clearly points out that our "want to" becomes the driver of our actions or lack of actions.Yes, I could have failed had I not embraced the notion that execution of a plan matters. Clay is right. His life challenges us to not settle, but to THRIVE. In doing so, we place ourselves in a position to light the darkness for others. It is in our reach to others that we truly maximize our existence on this planet. If I were still home in the Delta doing the same thing all those around me were doing, I seriously doubt if I would be able to light the pathway for myself or others. Today I am lighting the darkness as a businessman and writer, telling others what is possible for their lives. Clay's passionate plea for others to move beyond merely surviving comes from an honest place of caring. Why fail when you can THRIVE? Thank you, Clay, for not being afraid to step out beyond the ordinary and for inviting us along on your remarkable journey."

**— Clifton L. Taulbert**

*(The first African American west of the Mississippi to found a bank, a Pulitzer-Prize Nominated and Best-selling Author, long-time Clay Clark mentor and the President of the Building Community Institute President & CEO)*

I am the co-founder of five kids, the former "U.S. SBA Entrepreneur of the Year" for the State of Oklahoma, the founder of several multi-million dollar companies, and the host of the *Thrivetime Show* podcast, which has been number one overall on the iTunes business podcast charts 6 times. I have been a member of the *Forbes* Business Coach Council, an Amazon best-selling author and the host of the *Thrivetime Show*. Throughout my career I've co-founded / founded several successful businesses including:

» www.DJConnection.com

» www.EpicPhotos.com

» www.EITRLounge.com

» www.MakeYourLifeEpic.com

» Party Perfect (Which was purchased by Party Pro Rentals)

» TipTopK9 Franchising (I did not start TipTopK9 Dog Training, I co-founded TipTopK9 Franchising)

- » www.Thrive15.com
  (The interactive, online entrepreneurship school)

- » The Tulsa Bridal Association Wedding Show

Throughout my career, I have been featured in *Fast Company, Bloomberg, Forbes, Entrepreneur Magazine, PandoDaily,* and numerous other publications. I've been the speaker and consultant of choice for top brands throughout the country including: Hewlett Packard, Maytag University, Valspar Paint, and O'Reilly's Auto Parts. I'm also the co-founder of 5 children, the proud owner of thousands of trees, dozens of chickens, 13 cats, and one dog by the name of "Davis".

Since launching my ThrivetimeShow.com Podcast, the podcast has hit the top of the iTunes podcast charts 6 times and has featured interviews with hundreds of super successful entrepreneurs including those listed below and more:

 8x *New York Times* Best-Selling Author and Leadership Expert, John Maxwell

 Celebrity Chef, Entrepreneur, and *New York Times* Best-Selling Author, Wolfgang Puck

 Legendary Former Key Apple Employee-Turned-Venture Capitalist, Best Selling Author, Guy Kawasaki

 *New York Times* Best-Selling Co-Author of "Rich Dad Poor Dad", Sharon Lechter

 Senior pastor of the largest church in America with over 100,000 weekly attendees (Lifechurch.tv), Craig Groeschel

 One of America's most trusted financial experts who has written nine consecutive *New York Times* bestsellers with over 7 million books in print, David Bach

 Legendary Conservative Strategist, Roger Stone

 NBA Hall of Famer, David Robinson
(2x NBA Champion, 2-time Gold Medal Winner)

Senior Editor for *Forbes* and 3x Best-Selling Author, Zack O'Malley Greenburg

Most Downloaded Business Podcaster of All-Time (EOFire.com), John Lee Dumas

The 25th U.S. National Security Advisor, and Retired U.S. Army General, Michael Flynn

*New York Times* Best-Selling Author of "Purple Cow", and former *Yahoo!* Vice President of Marketing, Seth Godin

Co-Founder of the 700+ Employee Advertising Company (AdRoll), Adam Berke

*Emmy* Award-Winning Producer of the *Today Show* and *New York Times* Best-Selling Author of "Sh*tty Moms", Mary Ann Zoellner

*New York Times* Best-Selling Author of "Contagious: Why Things Catch On" and *Wharton* Business Professor, Jonah Berger

*New York Times* Best-Selling Author of "Made to Stick" and *Duke University* Professor, Dan Heath

International Best-Selling Author of "In Search of Excellence", Tom Peters

NBA Player and Coach, Muggsy Bogues (Shortest player to ever play in the league)

NFL Running Back, Rashad Jennings (and Winner of *Dancing with the Stars*)

Lee Cockerell (The former Executive Vice President of Walt Disney World, who once managed 40,000 employees)

Michael Levine (PR consultant of choice for Michael Jackson, Prince, Nike, Charlton Heston, Nancy Kerrigan, etc.)

*Billboard* Contemporary Christian Top 40 Recording Artist, Colton Dixon

Conservative Talk Pundit, Frequent *Fox News* Contributor, Political Commentator, and Best-Selling Author, Ben Shapiro

**See additional guests at:** ThrivetimeShow.com

Make Your Life Epic is a business consulting practice where I and my team coach 160 business owners every month in many different industries. The systems we recommend at Make Your Dog Epic are the same systems used in all industries to make them successful.

 *"When you WOW your clients they will refer you close to now." - Clay Clark*

Do you own a business? Well, I have a long track record of helping people to grow businesses using best-practice systems, processes, checklists, strategies, and moves I use.

Thousands of our client success stories can be found at: www.ThrivetimeShow.com. So, what is Make Your Life Epic? Make Your Life Epic is a best-practice business growth consulting company where I and my team coach 160 business owners in many different industries. The systems we use at Make Your Dog Epic are the same proven systems I teach our clients to make them successful.

**PAWS,**
for a Fun Fact

A dog can smell anywhere from 10,000 to 100,000X better than the average human. The part of the brain dedicated to smell is 40X larger in dogs than in humans.

*- MentalFloss.com*

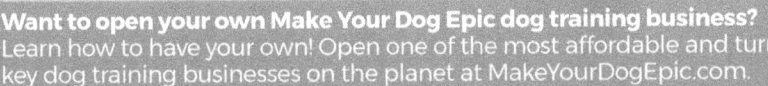

# READ CLAY CLARK'S BOOK(S):

Download Clay Clark's Books for Free at:
https://www.ThrivetimeShow.com/free-resources

## CLAY IS THE AUTHOR OF 20+ BOOKS INCLUDING:

**A MILLIONAIRE'S GUIDE TO BECOMING SUSTAINABLY RICH**
The World's Best Business Growth & Consulting Book: Business Growth Strategies from the World's Best Business Coach.

**F6 JOURNAL**
Meta Thrive Time Journal.

**BOOM**
The 14 Proven Steps to Business Success.

**WHEEL OF WEALTH**
An Entrepreneur's Action Guide.

**JACKASSARY**
Jackassery will serve as a beacon of light for other entrepreneurs that are looking to avoid troublesome employees and difficult situations. This is real. This is raw. This is unfiltered entrepreneurship.

**THE ENTREPRENEUR'S DRAGON ENERGY**
The Mindset Kanye, Trump and You Need to Succeed.

**MAKE YOUR LIFE EPIC**
Clay shares his journey and struggle from the dorm room to the board room during his raw and action-packed story of how he built DJConnection.com.

**THRIVE**
How to Take Control of Your Destiny and Move Beyond Surviving... Now!

**THE ART OF GETTING THINGS DONE**
Time-tested Super moves that you can use to create both the time freedom and financial freedom that most people only dream about.

**SALES DOMINATION**
Clay Clark is a master of selling and now he wants to teach you his proven processes, scalable systems and sales mastery moves in a humorous and practical way.

**ENTREPRENEURSHIP: SIMPLIFIED, AMPLIFIED, & VISUALIZED**
Throughout my career, I have been blessed to achieve tremendous success both as an entrepreneur and as a podcast host.

**WILL NOT WORK FOR FOOD**
9 Big Ideas for Effectively Managing Your Business in an Increasingly Dumb, Distracted & Dishonest America.

**HOW TO REPEL FRIENDS AND NOT INFLUENCE PEOPLE**
The epic whale of a tale featuring America's self proclaimed most humble male.

**DON'T LET YOUR EMPLOYEES HOLD YOU HOSTAGE**
This candid book shares how to avoid being held hostage by employees.

**IT'S NOT LONELY AT THE TOP**
15 Keys to achieving a successful, peaceful, and drama-free life. (3/4 of this book is handwritten by Clay Clark, himself).

**TRADE-UPS**
Learn how to design and live the life you love, how to find and create the time needed to get things done in a world filled with endless digital distractions, and more!

**IF MY WALLS COULD TALK**
The Notes, Quotes, & Epiphanies I've Written On Clay's Office Walls. (Hardcover).

**SEARCH ENGINE DOMINATION**
Learn the Proven System We've Used to Earn Millions.

**PODCAST DOMINATION 101**
This book will show you how to prepare, record, launch, and begin generating income from your podcast, all from your home studio!

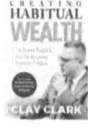
**CREATING HABITUAL WEALTH**
Are you looking for a proven and practical plan for achieving financial freedom? In this millionaire's guide, Clay Clark teaches the specific steps that you need to take in order to create habitual wealth.

**Want to open your own Make Your Dog Epic dog training business?** Learn how to have your own! Open one of the most affordable and turn-key dog training businesses on the planet at MakeYourDogEpic.com.

# A NOTE FROM OUR BOISE LOCATION, OWNER & TRAINER.

Thank you for striving to Make Your Dog Epic! No matter what, life is about goals, lessons, and learning. Isn't that such a great and wonderful thing!? It allows us to take things less seriously, and have some fun while away at lessons I didn't know that I had the opportunity to learn. I found that each dog provides us with new opportunities to learn and grow with them.

After training over 2,000 dogs over six years, we are still learning lessons to this day! Dogs are the most marvelous, inspiring, and heartwarming companions we could ever dream of. Your experience with training should be lessons for you and your dog, and there are always more lessons to learn. Learning, as most of us know, can take effort, patience, mistakes, time, energy, and a lot of help! It can seem daunting or confusing at times because it's so new! That is part of the process, and you will be glad you stayed the course! It also gives us understanding, patience, love, compassion, understanding, empathy, skills, tools, wisdom, knowledge, experience, results, and so much more!!

As the committed student you are, please remember, we are here for you and to help you! Whether it is something you want to hear or not, we are here to find solutions that work for you, your dog, and your lives together. Through practice makes progress, and we always want to enable you to progress together.

Your bond with your dog, the amount of freedom through discipline, and understanding will grow together, and we want to be part of that journey with you.

Every human is different, every dog is different, and every lifestyle is different. Our training can fit into whatever that combination looks like for your family.

You inspire us to continue to be better. You bring joy to our day by enabling us to spend time with you and your pups every day!

Our team is your support system and will always have your best interest at heart as long as you need us. We thrive and are delighted in seeing you and your dog have more understanding and joy together!

In your corner through this world of companion learning and joy,

Sincerely,
Darcy Denton-Heise

**PAWS,**
for a Fun Fact

According to Forbes, dogs are the most popular pet in the United States with 65.1 million U.S. households owning dogs. Approximately 49.5% of American households own a dog.

*- Forbes*
*(January 25, 2024.)*

# A NOTE FROM THE OWNER OF THE MAKE YOUR DOG EPIC OKLAHOMA LOCATIONS.

When you first start learning about dog training, sometimes it feels like the more you know, the less you know. There are thousands of dog trainers in America, all with different methods, training philosophies, training tools, and certifications. I have written this book from my experience having worked with thousands of dogs as a dog trainer, and from the teachings I have learned from Hollywood Dog trainers like Joel Silverman and Bryan Renfro, as well as trainers who changed my whole perspective on dog training like Tim Smith with 7F Dog Training, and others. Go to our website www.MakeYourDogEpic.com to see more information about our training method and philosophy. I understand there are many ways to train a dog, however, what we have done at Make Your Dog Epic is learn many different ways and methods of dog training and compressed it into our own transferable, teachable, repeatable, and scalable methodology we feel is the easiest way for both humans and dogs to understand. My passion is helping both you and your dog in the most repeatable and duplicatable way possible. I am honored you have put your trust in us to serve you and your dog. We do not take it for granted.

**Want to open your own Make Your Dog Epic dog training business?** Learn how to have your own! Open one of the most affordable and turn-key dog training businesses on the planet at MakeYourDogEpic.com.

My goal is to provide you with the best dog training experience possible! As well as a method that is extremely easy to transfer to anyone in the family. We refer to our method as Focused Based Positive Reinforcement Training and Methodology. When you sign up for our 50 Cent lesson we will show you how we train your dog transparently and right in front of you, so you can see our dog training best-practices and systems first-hand. However, this book is meant to lay a foundation for dog training no matter what method you use. Our ultimate goal at Make Your Dog Epic is to give dogs a better life through world-class and transferable dog training. In our society, dogs that listen get more freedom to go out in public or even just interact with the family and friends of dog owners. A goal for a lot of people is off-leash freedom with their dog. So they can go to places like the beach, public parks, or hiking trails. However, regardless of what your dog training goals are, we will get you there. We've structured this book so you can read it out of sequence if you wish. Feel free to jump around while reading the book. However, reading it in order will offer you significant benefits. In order to emphasize certain key themes and ideas, we have repeated certain concepts in the book. We hope you enjoy this book and journey on your way to having an EPIC dog!

Our Mission: Obedience but NEVER at the expense of the dog's personality. If you have to crush your dog's spirit to get it to listen, what's the point?

When reading this book, remember you can be as strict or as lenient with any commands or training as you want. My goal as a dog trainer is to get you to your specific goals!

(**Disclaimer**: This book is for real dogs not robot dogs.)

**Section One**

# Dog Training

# Our Commitment to Training

Our commitment is that we will be there for you and your dog even after you've completed your tailored dog training package. We train many dogs that have trained with other trainers, however, those who train with us never train anywhere else. Not necessarily because we are superior trainers, but because we will be there for the rest of your dog's life! With numerous dog trainers, training tools, methods, myths, and misconceptions out there, we are honored that you chose us to embark on this journey with you and your pup.

We will help you and your dog to achieve your specific goals. We understand that all dogs are unique, and everyone has distinct objectives with their pup. Whatever those goals may be, we will guide you and your dog down the path, until you reach them. We offer a money-back guarantee and we will NEVER shift blame to you if the training doesn't work. It will always be our responsibility!

No matter which training program you choose with us, group classes are included and you get lifetime phone support. That's because we want to be there for the entirety of your dog's life! Let's make your dog EPIC!

**CLAY CLARK**
Founder of
MakeYourDogEpic.com

**J.T. LAWSON**
Owner & Lead Trainer
MakeYourDogEpic.com
OKLAHOMA LOCATIONS

**PAWS**,
for a Fun Fact

"We all get good ideas at seminars and from books and business-building gurus. The problem is that most companies do not know how to identify and adapt the best ideas to their businesses. Implementation, not ideas, is the key to real success."

### - CHET HOMES

*(The best-selling author of "The Ultimate Sales Machine", and legendary business growth consultant.)*

**PAWS**, for a
Notable Quotable

"At Make Your Dog Epic, we believe that the
service, products, and solutions that we provide
should be so good that you'll want to work with us.
Having grown thousands of businesses, I believe
that anyone teaching highly manipulative sales
techniques, whether they have a beard and an eye
patch or not, is a modern pirate and a sick, twisted
freak. It does not matter to me whether someone
is suffering from "little-king" syndrome or they are
just a timid, cowardly, and weak force individual.
Any sales person who actually devotes time every
week to learn and train himself and his team
how to implement highly manipulative and high-
pressure sales techniques is not someone with
whom I would do business."

**CLAY CLARK**

# CHAPTER 1

# The Goal of a Dog Trainer

### JOKE TIME

*Q: What do you call a Frozen Dog?*

*A: Pupsicle*

I am writing this section from the heart because it genuinely hurts me that many dog trainers get this very wrong. Most dog trainers and dog training companies, I believe, started out with good intentions, but they lose their way somewhere down the road.

> **"YOU CAN NOT ONLY IMPROVE THE LIFE OF THE DOG THROUGH DOG TRAINING BUT YOU CAN LITERALLY SAVE DOGS' LIVES THROUGH DOG TRAINING."**

They started out with a passion for dogs. They love dogs, they care for dogs, they want the absolute best for them. Next, they start learning as much as they can, so they watch YouTube videos of training and try a couple of things. They possibly even bought a couple of dog training books or attended seminars. They start having success and get infatuated with the dog training realm. They start training other people's dogs or get a job as a dog trainer. They get really good, and they have a deep passion for dogs and people. They understand that behavioral issues are one of the top reasons dogs are surrendered to shelters. You can not only improve the life of the dog through dog training but you can literally save dogs' lives through dog training. My dog Riley is a shelter dog I got from the Williamson County Animal Shelter. She was their longest-stay there. She was there for over 6 months when I saw her. The whole time she was on the verge of being euthanized because of her behavior issues. She was very kennel aggressive and dog-aggressive. She is decent when it comes to people unless it's a crowd of kids or a grown man that's holding something resembling a pole or stick. She also has such a high toy drive that when people would come to visit her, she only cared about the toy instead of the new people. Not to mention, she was in a shelter in Alabama then surrendered to a shelter in Clarksville Tennessee, then she was given to Williamson County shelter as a stray. Needless to say, she has been through a lot. I got her when she was already 4 years old.

When I got her, she would not 'COME' no matter what anyone said or how loud they said it. She would jump on everyone, and she would immediately get aggressive around new dogs. She would resource guard. All these reasons are why she kept getting put back in shelters and not adopted. I was genuinely able to save her life through dog training. She does everything Achilles

does now. I still can't bring her to events because she gets overwhelmed in large crowds. However, she can now have a great life!

She gets off-leash freedom to play fetch, explore, play with Achilles, and jump in ponds. That is such a rewarding thing.

**Here she is on a fire hydrant!**

I give this story not to brag but to showcase that the goal of a dog trainer should be to SERVE. Serve the owner and the dog. I believe that is how most dog trainers start out. At some point down the line, it turns into wanting to be better than other dog trainers, speaking negatively about other dog trainers and owners, and using high-pressure sales tactics. They start worrying about comparing their own personal dog to other dog trainers' dogs and tearing them down instead of appreciating them for helping others.

For example, we recently did a home show, and there was another dog training company there. We had multiple people coming over to us saying they were talking badly about our company. They were more interested in talking badly about us than they were in serving their customers. No matter what realm of business you are in, you shouldn't have to talk badly about your competition to be able to get new customers. No matter how you train — not every single person in the world is going to like it, so you should be happy when someone finds a different trainer. The goal is happy dogs and clients. If we are booked out, we will recommend other trainers in town because we want them to find the help they need.

Trainers also have issues pushing their goals onto their clients. For example, I have trained and shadowed trainers that will sell a high-end package to a client that teaches the dog super long stays, 'COME' perfectly centered up and look the owner in the eye, 'HEEL OFF LEASH' and a bunch of other stuff for a 4-week boot camp. After the sales lesson, I asked, "Their biggest issues were jumping on people and barking. Wouldn't the cheaper package fix all

**PRO TIP:**

**MONEY IS AN AMPLIFIER. IF YOU ARE A PIECE OF CRAP BEFORE YOU MAKE A LOT OF MONEY, IT WILL JUST TURN YOU INTO A BIGGER PIECE OF CRAP. BE CAREFUL WHO YOU TEACH TO MAKE MONEY BECAUSE YOU'RE GOING TO AMPLIFY THEIR CHARACTER.**

these issues?" No exaggeration, they said, "Yeah, but did you see their cars? They can afford it." Every single sales lesson he had, he wouldn't actually listen to their problems; he would just try to get as much money out of them as possible. Or they think all dogs should be trained to their version of perfection and anything else is not acceptable. If any trainer believes differently, they will absolutely verbally bash them or turn into a keyboard warrior and bash them online.

I'm leaving names out of it because I don't believe in tearing down other trainers. But, I use this to hopefully educate new trainers on what NOT to do. The same trainer that I shadowed would use super dirty sales moves. I'll explain one to you. This s the move he taught all of his team to do. If a new customer says, "Well, I need to think about it or, I can't afford the package."— whatever the cost is. We will use $2,000 as an example. The response his team is supposed to say in a slow and low voice, "ahh ok, got it. Your dog currently doesn't 'COME' on command, which means they are probably going to get out the front door again. Next time, the chances are pretty high that it will get hit by a car. Is it fair to say your dog's life is worth less to you than $2,000?" He would guilt-trip them into buying packages, and a rule for their salespeople is that they cannot leave the lesson unless they get a 100% yes or a 100% no. They will sit in your house forever if all you do is say, "I have to think about it".

Make sure you don't forget your reason for starting to train dogs. Don't forget to serve people. Don't become a weak, feeble-minded little king who gets to their goals at the expense of others. Don't tear other people down to build yourself up. You should carry yourself with confidence but also be humble and remember your beginnings. Never screw over the people who put you on their back and helped you get to the top of the mountain, because if you do, it's a long way down. Strive for your goals but don't do it at the expense of others. Or simply put in the dog training world "don't bite the hand that feeds you". Even dogs understand that.

As a dog trainer, you're not only effecting the lives of dogs but the human's life as well. Think about how incredibly blessed you are to be able to do a job that's a paid hobby. You're paid to have fun and change lives. Keep that at the front of your mind at all times.

**PAWS**, for a
Notable Quotable

"You will never reach your destination if you stop and throw stones at every dog that barks."

**-WINSTON S. CHURCHILL**

*(The Prime Minister of the United Kingdom from 1940 to 1945 who defiantly stood up alone against Adolf Hitler and the Nazi party's quest to take over the world and to remove the Jewish people from the planet Earth.)*

# CHAPTER 2

# How Our Training System Was Created

THIS CHAPTER IS THE ABBREVIATED VERSION OF OUR WEBSITE PAGE. TO VIEW MORE, VISIT MAKEYOURDOGEPIC.COM. WE HAVE VIDEOS AS WELL AS PODCASTS THERE.

### JOKE TIME

*Q: What happens when you cross a dog with a lion?*
*A: You won't be getting any mail, that's for sure.*

I have come up with my own dog training system after years of training and learning from the best dog trainers in the industry. One of my strengths as a person is being coachable. When I go to learn from a trainer I brain dump all of the preconceptions I have about dog training. I try to be a sponge and soak up all of the knowledge they have to offer. I will constantly be on a journey to learn all there is about dog training. I have traveled the United States learning from some of the best trainers there are. With one goal in mind: soak up knowledge so I can then create a dog training system that not only gets the best results but is also the easiest for the dog and client to understand.

With our mission in mind, "Obedience but never at the expense of personality", I went on my journey. Most people don't know but there is no governing body over dog training, so the range of training varies so much.

This includes:

- » Positive reinforcement training
- » Clicker Training
- » Model Training
- » Mirror Training
- » Compulsion training
- » Alpha Dog Theory
- » Operant Conditioning
- » Discriminated Operant
- » Active Avoidance
- » Discriminated Omission
- » Passive Avoidance
- » Classical conditioning
- » Fear conditioning
- » Taste Aversion

There are so many different training methods. Not only that, but you have the different training tools that coincide with the methods. Such as:

- » Flat collar
- » Choke chains
- » Martingale collar
- » Prong collar
- » Gentle Leader
- » Pinch Collar
- » Haltis
- » Harnesses
- » Heeling sticks
- » Treats
- » All the different kind of treats
- » Clickers
- » Target sticks
- » Shock collars
- » E-collars
- » Whistles
- » All the different leashes

The list goes on and on. When first learning, it can be very confusing. I thought to myself while training, there has to be a better way. I found a trainer named Tim Smith, and his 7F

method of dog training is a foundational aspect of our training. I learned and continue to learn so much from Tim Smith. When I went out and learned from him, the information I gained GREATLY outweighed the cost of paying to learn from him. His underlying foundation in life and dog training is "Serving." When you are going through life, working with dogs, working with clients, in all you do

**"OUR MISSION: OBEDIENCE, BUT NEVER AT THE EXPENSE OF THE DOG'S PERSONALITY."**

you should be serving and through that give glory to God and be an Advocate for Christ. Here are a couple of pictures from my time training with him. He also taught me and my dog Achilles "Retrieve". If you ever see me with one of my dogs on a baseball field, I owe it to Tim Smith for teaching me how to teach it. He also thought it would be fun for me to take a bite from one of the dogs they were working with. I told them I wasn't scared but my face obviously tell you I lied HAH!

On our website is a fun video where we went to the Las Vegas strip and talked to people about different dog training techniques. We had a great time showing them all of Achille's tricks.

I have gained experience from having worked with thousands of dogs as a dog trainer, and from the teachings I have learned from Hollywood Dog trainers like Joel Silverman and Bryan Renfro, as well as trainers who changed my whole perspective on dog training like Tim Smith with 7F Dog Training and others. Go to our website www.MakeYourDogEpic.com to see more information about our training method and philosophy. I understand there are many ways to train a dog, however what we have done at Make Your Dog Epic is learn many different ways and methods of dog training and have compressed it into our own transferable, teachable, repeatable and scalable methodology that we feel is the easiest way for both humans and dogs to understand. My passion is helping both you and your dog in the most repeatable and duplicatable way possible.

My goal is to provide you with the best dog training experience possible that is the easiest to transfer to anyone in the family. We refer to our method as Focused Based Positive Reinforcement Training and Methodology. When you sign up for our 50 cent lesson we will show you how we train your dog transparently, and right in front of you so that you can see our dog training best-practices and systems first-hand. However, this book is meant to lay a foundation for Dog Training no matter what method you use. Our ultimate goal at Make Your Dog Epic is to give dogs a better life through world-class and transferable dog training. In our society dogs that listen get more freedom to go out in public or even just interact with the family and friends of dog owners. Dog owners that have a well-behaved and well-trained dog want to introduce their dogs to people! However, regardless of what your dog training goals are, we will get you there. We've structured this book so you can read it out of sequence if you wish. Feel free to jump around while reading the book. However, reading it in order will offer you significant benefits. In order to emphasize certain key themes and ideas we have repeated certain concepts in the book. We hope you enjoy this book and journey on your way to having an EPIC dog!

Our Mission: Obedience, but NEVER at the expense of the dog's personality. If you have to crush your dog's spirit to get it to listen, what's the point?

I also went to learn from Joel Silverman and Bryan Renfro at a dog training conference called "Dog Training For Film & TV Course" I learned a lot during my time training with them! It was much more than just dog training! I talked to them about the conference in the interviews below! Listen to find out more!

*This is a photo of me with Celebrity Dog Trainers Joel Silverman and Bryan Renfro*

# Who Is Joel Silverman?

The legendary dog trainer Joel Silverman was born and raised in Southern California. And at the very young age of just 13 years old, he trained his family dog, which was the first animal he ever trained. Shadow. During this period of celebrity dog trainer Joel Silverman's life, both he and his family decided to spend their summer vacations in beautiful San Diego, California, which is in southern California. During their vacation time spent together in San Diego, California the family would often visit SeaWorld. After spending multiple summers watching professional trainers riding orcas, Joel Silverman became very interested in whales and the whale trainers.

At just 16 years old, Joel Silverman got hired to be a trash collector at SeaWorld. However, after investing years of his time into assisting the trainers, Joel Silverman got hired as an actual trainer to work at the world-famous SeaWorld. Joel began training both Pacific and Atlantic bottle-nosed dolphins and California sea lions. However, eventually and after years and years of diligence and training, Joel Silverman became a trainer of orcas at SeaWorld!!!

In 1983, Joel Silverman began to change his focus to training the celebrity animals that people see when they watch movies, TV, film and commercials. In fact during the years of 1988 to 1992, Joel Silverman became the trainer for Dreyfuss from the TV series Empty nest. Then in 1989, Joel Silverman went on to host and create his first dog training video called Joel Silverman's Hollywood Dog Training Program. This dog training video went on to sell more than 300,000 videos!!! Then 10 years later, in 1999, Joel hosted his first TV series called "GOOD DOG U" which aired on animal planet for a decade from 1999-2009.

**Learn More About Joel Silverman Today At:**

www.JoelSilverman.net

## BUY JOEL SILVERMAN'S BOOKS TODAY:

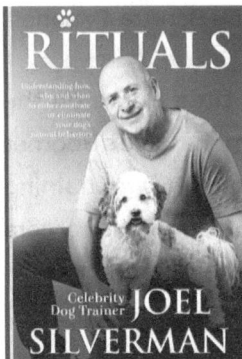  

### RITUALS

Understanding how, why, and when to either motivate or eliminate your dogs natural behaviors

Hardcover – July 15th, 2020

### WHAT COLOR IS YOUR DOG?

Train Your Dog Based on His Personality "Color" (Kennel Club Books)

Hardcover – June 16, 2009

### MORE WHAT COLOR IS YOUR DOG?

Understanding how, why, and when to either motivate or eliminate your dogs natural behaviors

Paperback – September 30, 2015

# Bryan Renfro

Bryan Renfro became known as one of the top dog trainers in all of Hollywood in the 1980s and 1990s. Bryan Renfro became well known and respected within the animal training industry for performing at the Animal Actors Stage at Universal Studios in the 1970s and 1980s where he personally trained Fred the Cockatoo from the Baretta TV series.

Bryan Renfro went on to train Bandit from Little House on the Prairie TV series and he even trained Boomer from the Here's Boomer TV series. Bryan actually performed with the animals he was training in the show. Bryan then went on to work on both sides of the camera when he went to work on the Rin-Tin-Tin TV series as a dog trainer. Bryan worked as a stuntman from 1988-1993 on the Rin-Tin-Tin TV series which was filmed up north in Toronto, California.

**Learn More About Bryan Renfro Today At:**

www.JoelSilverman.net/Bryan-Renfro/

## BUY BRYAN RENFRO'S BOOK TODAY:

**HARD WORK & DUMB LUCK:**

How a Road through Gangs, Drugs, and a Jungle Ended Up in Hollywood

March 9th, 2021

**PAWS,**
for a Fun Fact

Dogs sweat through
their paws instead of
their armpits.

**PAWS**, for a
Notable Quotable

"No one lives long enough to learn
everything they need to learn starting
from scratch. To be successful, we
absolutely, positively have to find
people who have already paid the price
to learn the things that we need to learn
to achieve our goals."

**BRIAN TRACY**

*(Best-Selling author, international speaker, sales trainer and
business growth consultant)*

# CHAPTER 3

# Dogs See In Pictures

### JOKE TIME

*Q: Where should you go if your dog is missing?*
*A: The lost and hound!*

I want to start with this chapter because if you understand this concept, you automatically become a better dog trainer no matter what method of dog training you choose to use. You will also become a better dog owner when you understand that dogs see in pictures. Dogs see in 'pictures', and they don't think rationally like you and I do. You should constantly keep this idea in your mind while engaged in dog training. The easiest way to explain this is to provide you with a couple of examples. First, is a common example in the dog training world. The mailman.

## EXAMPLE NUMBER 1: THE MAILMAN

The mailman comes to the door, the dog barks, and then the mailman leaves. In the dog's head, it thinks, "Wait a second, did I just do that?" Then, it happens again, and the dog thinks, "Oh, I did do that, awesome." Then it happens repeatedly, and every time it occurs, it seems to worsen. The dog starts to believe it just saved everyone in the house, the whole world, and is an honorary member of the Avengers now!

People typically use either positive or negative reinforcement in response to this behavior. Most opt for negative reinforcement because constant barking can be very annoying. It is also most people's default method of training. They may have read somewhere that they need to assert dominance in the household in order to have a well-behaved dog. Typically, they use dog training tools such as a prong collar, shock collar, fly swatter, choke chain, newspaper, squirt bottle, dad voice, etc.

Let's take the shock collar, for instance. When the mailman arrives and the dog barks, some people light the dog up with a shock collar. The dog is going to interpret this in one of two ways: either it understands and calms down, thinking, "Alright, I just need to chill out," or, more likely, because dogs see things in pictures and they do not think rationally, the dog associates the arrival of the mailman with its owner's anger and the shock from the collar. Now you have one or two outcomes from that. Either it gets worse and the dog starts barking louder, sooner, and more viscously, or the other outcome is the dog listens, but at the expense of the dog's personality, which is NEVER the goal.

## EXAMPLE NUMBER 2: DOGS GOING ON A WALK

When you're going on a walk and you see a dog, your dog growls a little bit. The other dog leaves, and in your dog's head, it thinks, "That dog just left because I growled, and now I've saved mom, the whole world, and I'm part of the Avengers!" Then this scenario repeats over and over, resulting in win after win. People typically resort to some form of either negative or positive reinforcement.

Most positive reinforcement trainers suggest a solution for this. You should get in front of the dog and redirect its attention to you. Then, when its attention is on you, you reward it. However, technically, you're rewarding bad behavior because the dog barks and you give it a treat. Even if your timing is perfect, your dog still associates barking at other dogs with getting a treat. This method might result in a reduction in constant barking and growling, but it doesn't entirely eliminate the behavior. Now, instead of just barking, it will bark, and then while barking, it will look at mom for a treat. Now, you need to have treats on you at all times, and your dog can never have a full stomach or they won't want treats, and the treats have to be super high value to overcome whatever the distraction level is.

Now, let's use the same example of going on a walk, but let's use a prong collar example. You have a trainer using a prong collar on the dog. Let's say the trainer does everything perfectly. He will turn and "pop" the dog hard enough to correct the dog. So now the dog walks perfectly for the trainer. This is very hard to transfer to clients, because now the trainer has to teach the client to have perfect timing. Also, maybe someone in the family doesn't have the strength or heart to use the prong collar. Well, now you're in a situation where the trainer will blame you for the training not working. Also, prong collars only work if you are attached to the dog with a leash. If you have no leash, you have no "authority".

*To see how we fix this issue, skip down to the anxiety and aggression chapter of the book.*

**First Picture:** If you say 'COME' to the dog, and every time you make the dog come into the 'HEEL' position on your side. The dog sees in that 'picture' so then training it to come in straight and look at you is a completely different picture for the dog. Maybe you are teaching 'PLACE'. Well, it typically takes teaching place on 10 different spots before your dog will start to associate any elevated boundary as place.

**Second Picture:** If you teach, 'COME' and 'SIT' in front of you. But then while you're walking away you say come and the dog is allowed to run past you. You are mixing two different pictures with one command.

**First picture:** move towards me and you must sit in front of me

**Second picture:** move towards me, but you can do whatever you want.

When you do this and you're using the same command for both pictures, the first picture starts to get really blurry for the dog, and they don't know how to handle it. The solution is to label the second picture "let's go", and it can be as ugly as it needs to be. But you want to be strict on that first command because 'COME' is the command that's going to save the dog's life if it starts running into a street, or if you're hiking and there is a stray animal. 'COME' needs to mean you come and sit close enough to me that I can touch you without moving my feet, preferably touching me.

**PAWS**,
for a Fun Fact

The average dog's mental age is equivalent to that of a two-and-a-half year old child judging by the number of words, signs, and signals the dog can understand.

*- SafariVet.com*

**PAWS**, for a
Notable Quotable

"I've been screwed, I've had millions of dollars
embezzled from me, and I've had ungrateful
partners push me out of their businesses after I've
helped them to grow their business by 18x without
apology, simply to increase their income. At the end
of the day, we must all choose to become bitter or
better, or over time we will become so cold that we
should wear a sweater."

**-CLAY CLARK**

*(6X iTunes chart-topping podcast host and the
co-creator of five human kids.)*

# CHAPTER 4

# Puppy Training

**JOKE TIME**

*Q: Why do dogs float?*
*A: Because they're good buoys!*

This chapter is primarily for people who want to start a good foundation with their puppies. This chapter of the book is filled with extra tips and tricks you can use before training with us. You could think of these tips and tricks as "hacks" to use before we start training your fur baby. Also, tips if you're thinking about getting a dog or how to find a good veterinarian near you, etc. This doesn't encompass all things puppies, but it's a good start. Your Make Your Dog Epic trainer can answer any specific questions you have!

## KENNEL TRAINING

This topic is typically emotionally hard on dog owners. At Make Your Dog Epic, we do not use kennels as punishment—EVER. We use it as a training tool and a "den" for dogs. When it comes to kennel training, you can either do fast or slow. The choice is yours on what you feel like is the best option for your dog. There is no correct method. I tend to lean towards doing it fast with all my dogs unless I have an extremely anxious dog. Now you might be thinking, "I NEVER plan on putting my dog in a kennel. So I don't need to kennel train them." I understand, however, there are going to be times when you have no choice but to put your dog in a kennel. If that happens and your dog isn't kennel-trained, it is going to make it EXTREMELY tough for the dog. Here are some examples:

1. If you have to leave your dog at the veterinarian.
2. If you have to board your dog somewhere.
3. Potty training.
4. If you have them in a kennel while traveling in the car.
5. If they have to fly on an airplane.
6. If they need to be in a kennel at a hotel room.
7. If your dog gets injured and the veterinarian says you need to keep your dog in a kennel so it doesn't reinjure itself.
8. If you leave your dog at the groomers.

The examples can go on and on, but you get the point. Your dog is going to live a very long life. Thus, the chances of it never needing to be in a kennel is extremely low. So, if you don't want the first time kennel training your dog to be a traumatic time for it, I fully suggest you kennel train your dog early on in its life.

Here is how you get them to like their kennel. You can feed them inside the kennel with the door shut. They get 15 minutes to eat. If they don't eat, then the food goes back up, and they don't see it until their next time to eat. You might have to do this 3 or 4 times. The reason you're doing this is because we are teaching the dog to control their emotions and self-regulate their anxiety. The first couple times they might not eat. But, eventually they will think to themselves "I hate being in this kennel... However, I'm starving." They will take a metaphorical deep breath, relax, and start to eat. In return, this will over time teach them that when they feel like this, they need to take that deep breath. It will teach them to regulate their emotions.

You may also put them in the kennel randomly throughout the day for 30 seconds, 3 minutes, 10 min, etc., not just when you are going to leave the house for hours. That way your pup doesn't think they are going to be in the kennel for hours anytime they are put in it.

You don't want anything in the kennel the dog can chew up. Only put toys in the kennel that are not a choking hazard for the dog. Freedom is earned, not given, so if you want to put a blanket in the bottom that's fine. This is how you do it. You need to put the blanket in there for a couple minutes, and come back and check if it's chewed up. If you see that it's chewed up, you need to take it out and the dog loses blanket privileges. If it's not chewed up, then leave the blanket in for a little longer, and progressively extend the time. There are a LOT of dogs who don't get anything allowed in their kennel. This is normal, so don't be discouraged if you can't leave stuff in there. I honestly suggest people don't put anything in the kennel because we want it to be a place the dog can relax and shut its brain off. However, I know many people are going to put things in the kennel anyway, so I might as well tell you how to do it safely.

The dog "liking" their kennel and the dog going into the kennel everytime you ask are completely different things. You can work on teaching your dog to like the kennel. Our team will teach "kennel" and teach your dog to go there the first time you ask.

## PLAY BITING

Most dogs will grow out of this phase by the age of 5 to 7 months old. The ease of fixing this issue usually depends on the specific breed of the dog. Herding breeds and working breeds are typically harder to fix. There are a couple tricks to fixing this.

One that can work almost instantly or your dog won't care at all, is the yelping method. If your dog bites too hard and you give a high-pitched yelp as though you've been hurt, it can stop it instantly. On the other hand, your dog might just assume you're playing and play more rough. This method is not very reliable, but because some dogs care and it takes no time to do so, you might as well give it a try because sometimes it works wonders.

Another option, which is tedious, but the most common method, is replacing your hand for a toy. As soon as they start to bite you, move your hand away and replace it with a toy. I would not use treats during this. You will technically be rewarding the bad behavior. The dog bites your hand, you replace your hand with a toy and then give the dog a treat, it will start to learn when they bite your hand, they get a treat. When doing this method, if it is black and white for the dog, it will be easier for the dog to understand. If you allow play biting sometimes, but not others it can be confusing. The moment your dog starts biting on you, give it a toy. If your dog still tries to bite you, stop play time. Just walk away.

These are all methods which can work, but they can take a long time. When we work with your dog, we will teach "OFF" (which means move away physically and mentally, but not that your dog is not in trouble) which is important because I don't want your dog to think you're mad or playing is bad. Just "hey knock it off". However, the options above can work until we work with your dog.

## STORY TIME

My dog Achilles is a Belgian Malinois and his dad did Mondioring in France, so he was bred to bite. Achilles loves to play fight, and communicates through his mouth while nibbling. If you have a dog like Achilles and you try to push them off, run away, or yelp, he will immediately think you're playing and comes at you way harder. With a working breed, they need something to do. You need to replace yourself with a toy. This is harder because you're more fun to play with. You move and make sounds. You get them tug toys, or some type of toy that you can put in their mouth.

## HEALTH CARE

There is no medical advice found in this book. Go get this advice from your veterinarian. However, I can give some advice on how to find a veterinarian you can trust. Veterinarians are a lot like dog trainers in the sense when you talk to them, they all will have varying opinions on a lot of things. To sum this section up: keep trying new veterinarians until you find one you can trust. I'll give you an example from personal experience. When I first moved to Nashville, I did not have a veterinarian that I trusted yet. My dog Achilles was having issues itching all the time, and he had this weird spot on his nose that appeared randomly. I went to three different veterinarians to get opinions, and all three gave different answers.

The first one I picked, because it was the closest to where I lived. They told me I needed to change his diet, and they needed to sedate him to do surgery to remove the spot from his nose.

The second one, I picked because I asked a friend of mine at the gym who they used. They said that they needed to put medication on the spot and see if that healed it, and come back in a couple weeks to follow up with it to make sure it wasn't cancer. For the itching, they said I should take him to the dermatologist (which happened to be a parent company for that veterinarian).

The last veterinarian I picked, because it was close and had the most positive Google reviews. This veterinarian said to just leave the nose alone, and it would be gone in a couple of weeks. If it got worse, to come back in. They also said, based on what I told them, it couldn't possibly be the food causing it, so switching food wouldn't work. He needed a shot of Cytopoint.

I used my intuition and used the veterinarian that made the most logical sense to me. When first looking, you want to visit multiple veterinarians and decide for yourself who is best for your furbaby!

## LITTERMATES

If you have littermates, this can be a great thing. However, you will want to separate them as much as you can. The reason being is littermates are very prone to having severe separation anxiety. I once had a first 50 cent lesson with two German shepherds who were littermates. We met at a park, and if you pulled them farther than 6 feet from each other, they both would start to thrash on the leash, bark, whine, and sled dog towards each other. The parents said if they tried to walk one of them and leave the other at home, the one left at home would destroy the blinds and scratch at the front door while barking and whining for the whole neighborhood to hear. The dog outside wasn't quite as bad, but it wouldn't even want to go on the walk and It would pull towards the house. We helped them a lot, and now they can leave one at the house and go on walks, and they are both happier and living a better life, however, most of this could've been avoided in the early stages.

Basically the advice here is simplified, if you have littermates, separate them as much as possible for the first year of their life. You will 100% need to kennel train them. Refer to the earlier section in this chapter if you need more information on kennel training. Here is a list of ways to separate them: Have them eat and sleep in separate kennels which are in separate rooms. You might be thinking this is extreme but you must get them used to doing things without seeing or hearing the other one. When you do this over and over it becomes just a way of life.

Every chance you get, take one with you while you leave the other one. If you go on a walk, take one at a time. If you go to a friend's place, take one and leave the other. You do not have to do this every single time, and obviously they are allowed to do stuff together but do it as often as possible. The goal is to teach them that being away from each other is a normal way of life.

The most important part of this is having them eat separately. I'm going to walk you through how and why to do it. The way you do this is to put them in their kennel in separate rooms, put the food in the kennel, and close the kennel. They get 15 minutes to eat. If they don't eat, then the food goes back up, and they don't see it until their next time to eat. You might have to do this 3 or 4 times. The reason you're doing this is because we are teaching the dog to control their emotions and self regulate their anxiety. The first couple times they might not eat, but eventually they will think to themselves "I hate being in this kennel land, I really need to be with my sibling...However, I'm starving." They will take a metaphorical deep breath, start to relax, and begin to eat. Over time, I will teach them that when they feel like this, they need to take that deep breath.

## ANXIETY

Anxiety will mostly be handled in the Aggression and Anxiety Chapter, but I want to help you make sure you're not inadvertently training your puppy to have anxiety. Your dog does not understand English (or Spanish) so refer to the chapter - 10 Virtues of dog training for more on this. If you put your dog in a kennel or separate room and they start whining and you go back to them they immediately learn "Oh, when I whine and throw a fit my parents come back to me." You need to ignore the dog when they are whining. The younger you start the dog, the easier it will be. You're creating the picture for the dog (refer to chapter 1). So if you put them in the laundry room, and it starts scratching at the door and whining and barking and you come back in and say "hey buddy you're fine. Dad is right outside", the dog doesn't understand what you're saying. All it understands is it whined and it got dads attention. On the other hand, if you come back in and yell at the dog, it starts to think "Dang every time I go in the kennel, dad yells at me. I really hate being put in here."

When you come home and leave, do not make it a big deal. I would ignore the dog for a couple minutes, and then you can play with them and be excited. If not, you're training the dog to jump on you and go crazy the moment you walk through the door. Which might be cute while they are small, but it won't be when they are grown and you want your grandma to come over, but Fluffy is trained to jump on everyone.

**Example:** Think about when you leave the house and you say to your dog:

> **Mom:** "Oh my gosh, Fluffy, mom's going to work. Have a great day. I'll miss you! See you when I get home!"

> **What the dog hears:** "Bye, Fluffy, mom is going to work and I might die. Hopefully I make it home if bad things don't happen".

> Then after work you come in super excited

> **Mom:** "Oh my gosh, Fluffy, how are you! I missed you so much".

**What the dog hears:** "Oh no, Fluffy. I can't believe I made it home! I almost died, there are so many monsters out there. Please freak out because this is a big deal".

Even if the dog magically understands English, you're still conditioning the dog to go crazy every time you leave and come home. Your dog starts to think that's what's expected.

## PUPPY HABITS, GROWN-UP TRAITS

You must understand that the behaviors that are cute and adorable while they are little will most likely not be adorable when they are big. For example, jumping and whining to get in your lap. Think about a 3 month old Husky puppy.

This is possibly one of the cutest puppies. When they are jumping on you and whining, it's very cute and adorable and it melts your heart. So you give them attention each time they do it. However, that cute little puppy that was about 10-20 pounds turns into this.

Which is still cute and adorable, but now you've taught it that if it jumps, it gets attention. So now when grandma comes over, you have a dog that jumps on her for attention.

## STORY TIME

When I got Achilles, I gave him a couple weeks without training because I wanted to take that time to bond with him and give him a chance to adjust before immediately training him. I took him to see my family because they wanted to meet him. He immediately ran over to my grandma and jumped on her. I had to catch her before she hit the ground. She said "Some dog trainer you are," she was not very pleased hah! Even though he was a cute little dog at that weight and size, having a baby Belgian Malinois is like owning a baby velociraptor. I want to show you three progressions, which are all photos before he was a year and a half old.

**He went from this:**

**To this:**

**To this:**

Now at any of these sizes, jumping is an issue, but especially at almost full grown.

Think about all the things your dog is doing as a puppy and ask yourself when it's happening, if it will still be cute when they are older. Bitting, tugging at your pants, counter surfing, chewing up things, barking, etc. Some people think the behaviors will stop once they are older and have less energy. Maybe that's somewhat true. However, some dogs have puppy-like energy until they are 9 or 10 depending on the breed.

## MYTH

If I get my dog neutered, they will be better behaved. I can not stress this enough that it's not true in any way. Yes, maybe it lowers your dog's testosterone a little bit. But it's not magically going to get your dog to listen better or stop being aggressive towards other dogs. Never neuter your dog if it is purely for obedience reasons. Never neuter a man for obedience reasons either.

## SOCIALIZATION

Socialization at an early age is very important. Doing it correctly is even more important. NUMBER 1 RULE of socialization is absolutely no dog parks. Refer to the dog park section for more information on this. You want to get your dog around other people and dogs as often as possible.  Just no dog parks.

We will start with getting your dog around other dogs first. It's very important you do this in a safe way. It only takes one dog to attack your dog for your dog to have that 'picture' forever. Find friends who have friendly dogs, and you all can have doggy play dates with them. You can also set it up to where you pass them on walks, and let your dog say hi to them. This way, they get used to other dogs being friendly.

With humans, a trick is when you have people over or when you are out in public, you can give the other people treats. Then when your dog walks up to them and says "hi", have them give your dog a treat. If you have a more timid dog, this might take longer. If you have an already outgoing dog, the people might not even need treats and just petting the dog will be plenty of excitement.

I will address something that I am sure someone out there is arguing with me on. "When training you want your dog focused on you. If you do these steps the dog will be more focused on other dogs and people than you and you will have a hard time getting the dog to focus on you." My rebuttal to this would be "That's true. However, it is always easier to train a dog to focus on

**PAWS,**
for a Fun Fact

Your dog can smell 40x
better than you can.
*- MontecitoPetHospital.com*

you than it is to train a dog who doesn't like people or dogs, to like people or dogs. Every single time" Do not worry about this. Obedience is always fixable. Anxiety and aggression is not. When in doubt, I would always rather have your dog like humans and dogs "too much"

## DESENSITIZATION

Desensitization early is important. You want to think of all the typical things you know of dogs not liking and do that with your puppy. Sounds strange, but the more you do it, the more it's a normal thing and not some massive event. For example: Car rides, tail, ear, paws, nails, getting in the tub, being in the kennel, being held, walking with other people, staying with other people. Anything you can think of that you've seen dogs not like. You want to take your dog with you as often as you can in the car that way they are used to it. I'll use my dog Achilles as an example. While he was a puppy, I would take him on car rides all the time. While we were driving, I would mess with his ears, feel his paws, as well as hold them. I would also randomly hold his tail. I know he is a Belgian Malinois and was bred to do MondioRing. That's what his dad and mom did. So he has all those genetic traits however, I needed him around kids and people. I was very intentional about doing things like randomly putting him in the bathtub and kennel training him so he was used to it. The more you do each thing the more normal it becomes. Now kids lay on top of him and smother him and he is completely fine!

**PAWS**, for a
Notable Quotable

"Drifting, without aim or purpose, is the first cause of failure."

### -NAPOLEON HILL

*(The best-selling author of Think & Grow Rich.)*

**PAWS**, for a
Notable Quotable

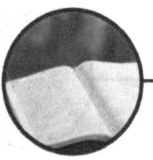

"He that walketh with wise men shall be
wise: But a companion of fools shall be
destroyed."

**- PROVERBS 13:20**

*(King James Version)*

# CHAPTER 5
# Potty Training

**JOKE TIME**

*Q: Which dog breed is guaranteed to laugh at all of your jokes?*
*A: A Chi-ha-ha!*

## THE GUIDE TO PUPPY POTTY TRAINING: 9 STEPS TO SUCCESS

Unless you hate your life and want your home to smell like dog excrement, potty training your puppy is a crucial step in raising a well-behaved and happy puppy. Establishing a routine, using positive reinforcement, and understanding your puppy's cues are the keys to success. In this guide, we will walk you through a 9 step process to make potty training easier and more effective, along with some do's and don'ts to ensure a smooth journey. Remember, patience and consistency are key! Good luck! We understand potty training is one, if not the most frustrating part of dog training. Our goal is to simplify the process for you. The process is tedious, and possibly annoying, but WAY less annoying than picking up pee and poop everyday!

**PAWS,**
for a Fun Fact

Watch your step! It only takes one step to know if your dog needs more potty training.

# 9 Steps to Potty Training:

### STEP #1- BEGIN YOUR DAY EARLY

Start your day by taking your puppy outside in the morning. On average, puppies can hold their bladder one hour per month of age, so this morning trip sets the tone for the day and helps establish a routine. This is dependent on the dog's age, breed, and size. There is no one size fits all for the amount of time for puppies.

### STEP #2- LET THEM CHOOSE THEIR SPOT

Allow your puppy to choose their potty spot during this morning outing. Have them on leash to keep them from distractions. They can lead you but if they start eating stuff or playing with stuff keep them moving. They will mark this spot, and it will become their designated potty area during training. However, keep them on a leash to ensure they cannot get too distracted. Each puppy is unique, so let them explore and pick their preferred potty spot. Once they find their spot you should continue taking them to that spot every single time.

### STEP #3- NOW DON'T LET THEM CHOOSE THEIR SPOT

After those first couple take outs with your new puppy, now you need to start taking them to the same area every time. Have them on a leash so they can not get super distracted. When they get into a habit of going to the same spot over and over, it will start to become easier, and easier. They should only get a maximum of 10-15 minutes to go potty.

## STEP #4- POSITIVE REINFORCEMENT

Keep repeating "go potty" until they do. Praise your puppy enthusiastically every time they use the designated potty spot. You can also offer a treat to reinforce the behavior and make it more enjoyable. Be Careful with this step and make sure you are rewarding the correct behavior. Do not reward them when they get back inside. Reward them right away. Caveat to this rule: if your dog loves treats so much they won't go potty because they are so focused on you, then do not use treats.

## STEP #5- IF THEY DON'T GO POTTY

This is the most tedious part and will test your patience a lot. It is also the most vital. If your puppy does not go potty, you need to bring the puppy back in and immediately have it go in its kennel. The kennel should not be a bad thing at this point because you have made it a fun place. Refer to the puppy chapter of this book for more information on kennels.

## STEP #6-  KENNEL SOILING

If your kennel is too spacious and the dog can pee and poop on one side and sleep on the other side then the kennel is too big. Consider getting a smaller kennel or using partitions to limit space. Yes, this means a couple times you will need to clean pee off your dog.

## STEP #7-  KENNEL SOILING: THE BAD NEWS

If your dog's kennel is small enough and it's peeing all over itself, that means it genuinely can not hold it and you need to let the puppy out more often. If you're letting your dog out frequently and it continues doing this after weeks of training, unfortunately you may have one of the very rare cases of a dog that simply does not care about it. Talk to a trainer if this is the case.

## STEP #8- NEVER EVER

Never rub your dog's nose in the mess. They do not know! They only know that you came home and are pissed. The dogs timing is VERY important! If it does not happen immediately after the dog will not associate them going potty in the house with the punishment. Even if you manage to time it perfectly and the dog understands, it's not a good way to punish them because this will just create sneaky dogs. You will just teach the dog to do it where you won't see them. Which means now they will do it in the other room, the closet, and even under the bed.

## STEP #9- CREATE A SCHEDULE

The more strict you are on a schedule, the quicker the potty training will happen. Do not free feed or it will be IMPOSSIBLE to create a schedule with your dog. Feed them at designated times, and only let them get 20 minutes to eat. If they don't eat, the food goes up until the next designated feeding time. If the dog is used to free feeding, it might not eat the first couple times. Your dog will start to understand. The key thing to watch is how soon the dog is using the bathroom after and create the potty schedule accordingly.

# FREQUENTLY ASKED POTTY TRAINING QUESTIONS

### 1. How Do I Recognize When My Puppy Needs to Go?

Watch for signs like whining, barking, restlessness, pacing, sniffing, or circling. These cues indicate your puppy needs a potty break. You should also create a schedule with the dog. You should know how long it takes for them to digest their food.

### 2. How Long Does Potty Training Take?

Potty training duration varies depending on age, breed, and the individual dog itself. It can take a few weeks to up to six months for complete potty training.

### 3. How Should I Handle Mistakes?

React calmly and never punish your puppy for accidents. Interrupt them with a loud clap or a noise, but not an angry yell if you catch them in the act, and take them to the designated potty spot. If your dog knows the "OFF" command, you may use that as well. Clean accidents thoroughly to remove odors. Using punishment will only teach them to be more sneaky and do it when you're not watching or in the closet. Never leave copious amounts of urine and dog feces around your home, never live with twelve dogs, and don't become a hoarder. Also, choose now to never become weak, feeble, frail, soft, wimpish, slight, tender, lame, wimpy, passive aggressive, and a double-minded, back-stabbing, greedy person.

### 4. Can I Use Potty Pads?

While potty pads can be convenient in some situations, using them can confuse your dog. It's best to prioritize outdoor potty training to avoid mixed signals. A potty pad feels a lot like carpet or a rug so it can be confusing. If you are in an apartment complex with a balcony, you may use them there. However, never use them inside. Unless you have a small breed that will never be potty trained because their bladder is genuinely too small.

### 5. Shouldn't We Be Getting Results Faster?

It's essential to understand potty training takes time and patience. Some dog owners expect instant results, but every dog is unique, and the learning process varies. Don't be discouraged by occasional setbacks; consistency is the key to success.

## MYTH CORRECTION

> "MY DOG KNOWS HE DID SOMETHING BAD
> BECAUSE WHEN I COME HOME AND SEE THE
> MESS AND LOOK AT HIM HIS EARS ARE BACK OR
> HE GOES AND HIDES IN HIS KENNEL."

# WRONG!

Your dog understands your blood pressure is rising and you're upset. You have conditioned your dog to be scared and run to its kennel when it senses this.

**Conclusion:**

Potty training is a journey that demands patience, consistency, and the right approach. By following these tips and dispelling common myths, you can successfully potty train your dog. Remember that each dog is unique, so adapt your training to their specific needs. If you require further guidance, reach out to our team and we will help guide you through the process. Potty training can be a rewarding experience, strengthening the bond between you and your four-legged companion.

**PAWS,**
for a Fun Fact

Dogs sniff rear ends as their way of asking "who are you and how have you been?".

*- MentalFloss.com*

**PAWS**, for a
Notable Quotable

"All successful people men and women are big dreamers. They imagine what their future could be, ideal in every respect, and then they work every day toward their distant vision, that goal or purpose."

**- BRIAN TRACY**

*(Best-selling author, world-class trainer, motivational speaker and sales trainer.)*

# CHAPTER 6
# 10 Sins Of Dog Training

**JOKE TIME**
*Q: Where do dogs hate to shop?*
*A: The flea market!*

## #1 - LEASHES THAT EXTEND

I understand the appeal of leashes that extend. Before I started my dog training journey, I used extendable leashes all the time. You can give your dog more freedom to potty or play when you want, or you can keep the dog close if you need to. Which sounds GREAT! However, think about what the dog is seeing. Your dog thinks "sometimes when I pull I get to go farther away and I get to go where I want. I'll just start pulling all the time!" Now you have accidentally taught your dog to pull on the leash.

## #2 - HARNESSES

*Disclaimer: I understand that some dogs need to be on a harness for a reason that your veterinarian said. If that is the case ignore this.*

For the majority of people, they typically switch to a harness because the dog is pulling so hard its choking itself or they feel like it gives them more control. Or they use the front of the Harness because it mitigates the pulling a little bit. Think about any sled dog ever. They all wear harnesses because they can pull with absolutely no restraint.

They have the collar attached but it's for "direction" to keep them in the straight line.

You have good intentions, but you're creating a sled dog. Dog trainers use harnesses to make dogs want to pull harder towards things. They use harnesses so the dog can pull, but there is no negative restraint.

## #3 - DOG PARKS

Dog parks are the one thing I would say most dog trainers are on the same page about. They are an absolute NO! I'm going to give you real life examples of things I have heard in our 50 cent lessons.

I did a 50 cent first lesson with a 3 year old Schnauzer. These are their actual words.

> **Them**: "We want to work on obedience and I guess socialization. We think socialization is under control. We are taking him to the dog park. It's gone pretty well. He has been in a couple dog fights, but we know its just about repetition and practice. But we are struggling a lot with his obedience"

> **Me**: "You say a couple fights. How many is that? Tell me about it."

> **Them**: "Well It's like 7-8 ish fights. Its for sure less than 15. But he hasn't gotten into a fight in like half a year."

> **Me**: "When was the last time you went to the dog park?"

> **Them**: "About sixish months ago."

This is a real conversation of many that I wish I was making up. But their dog has gotten into many dog fights at the dog park and they think the solution is to keep going to the dog park.

Now, you might be thinking "Well sure that person needs to stop going to the dog park obviously but my dog isn't aggressive so it's fine". This issue with this is it just takes one dog to attack your dog for your dog to be aggressive or skittish forever. Dogs don't think rationally like humans do, they see in pictures. If you walk into a store and someone randomly punches you in the face as a human you can think "ok well that sucks but it's not what's going to happen every time." With dogs you have fight or flight and they don't think rationally. So depending on the dog, sometimes it just takes once. If the dog is confident it will think "I'm going to attack these dogs before they can attack me" with a non confident dog they think "at any moment one of these dogs could attack me"

Instead of just talking about how bad dog parks are, I'm going to give you solutions to the 3 main reasons people go to dog parks. I understand you want to get your dog socialization, exercise, and give the dog off leash freedom.

> **Off leash freedom:** You fix that with one of two solutions. Option one is to train the dog so their "COME" command is proofed. That's how you get full off leash freedom. Option two is find someone else that has a yard big enough you can go where your dog can run around.

> **Exercise**: This one has unlimited solutions. Dog Treadmill, walks, fetch, hire a dog walker, hire a squirrel trainer to have it run in a circle around the yard while your dog chases it. (Just kidding PETA)

**Socialization**: When in doubt, talk to a reputable trainer about this one. This one is very different on a case by case basis.

You can get a group of people together who have dogs that all get along. They can all play together. Just make sure any dogs that have not met before, are introduced slowly to each dog. Don't just throw them into the group, it can be very overwhelming. This is a great solution if you love all the things about the dog park. Have a group of people with dogs you trust, and let them all play together. The main issue with dog parks is too many dogs at a time and people bring aggressive dogs all the time. You don't want their negligence to affect your dog's life.

## #4 - STARTING WITH HIGH VALUE THINGS

This one isn't a major deal, it's just a pro tip with treat training. Think of treats and toys from now on as high and low value. For example a dog that doesn't like toys. The toy no matter what toy is low value because he doesn't care about it. I'll use my dog Achilles for example because he is a good mix. My other dog Riley is psycho for all toys and treats. For her the best toy is a tennis ball but it is only slightly above everything else.

### WITH ACHILLES IT GOES LIKE THIS:

- **Other animals like goats, chickens, squirrels.**

- **Steak or chicken**

- **His dog food**

- **Playing with dogs**

- **Playing rough with dad**

- **Kids**

- **The green squishy fetch ball**

- **Other people**

- **Water buffalo horn**

- **Other toys**

*Scarcity breeds value in dogs.* What do I mean by this? If I leave frisbees out all the time where the dog has access to it, they start to lose their value. However, if I only bring the frisbee out for short spurts like when the dog is training, then they start to crave the frisbee even more.

I'll explain this in human terms. When I went through basic training for the Army, I went 4 months without seeing my phone. For two months I never heard music. Then we took a bus to a training exercise and the driver played music. I realized in the moment how much I valued and took music for granted. The music on the bus had my complete attention. I started listening very closely to the lyrics, and how the beat and chords in the music made me feel. This was a massive endorphin release. Before basic training music would just be in the background and wasn't a big deal. Kind-of like when you were a kid, coloring books were AWESOME! Until you discovered video games and smartphones. It's the same for dogs if the thing is always around it loses value. A big mistake that people make in treat training is they start with super high value things like steak but now you're stuck using that every time because it means more than any other treat. However, overall it means less because it's readily available. But because the squirrel is not always there, it already meant more to the dog than steak did. Now when the dog sees the squirrel it could care less about the steak, it just wants the squirrel.

## #5 - LABELING BEFORE IT'S CLEAR

Think about how many times you said "sit" the first time you tried to get your dog to sit. Most people say it like 4 times before the dog sits. That's because they inadvertently taught the dog that the command is "sit sit sit sit". The dog thinks on the 4th command if ever then it has to sit. Or it thinks it can sit whenever it feels like it. One thing that we do differently at Make Your Dog Epic is we don't label commands until they are clear. We teach the dog the action first and have them do it until they understand what we want from them. Then we label it. (Label means to overlay a word with an action) The reason we do this is because our goal in training is: Clarity for the dog, least amount of bad reps as possible, and the dog listens for the first time everytime to commands.

## #6 - ASKING AND NOT TELLING

This goes along with the last section. I am absolutely positive you have done this or heard someone else do it. They say in a super soft voice "can you sit?" and it sounds like a question. Or they ask in a baby voice. You should never raise your voice (unless your dog is far away obviously). However, the commands should be you telling the dog what to do not asking. There are several reasons for this behavior. Firstly, if you're constantly asking the dogs, they're likely to ignore you. However, the primary reason is that if you always ask in a gentle tone but suddenly switch to a stern voice, particularly by the fourth command, your dog might start feeling as though it's in trouble. This can lead to a loss of its personality or a fear of training altogether, as the dog associates training with the expectation of being scolded by its owner.

## #7 - OVER USING "GOOD"

If you use good to "release the dog" and use good to tell them they are doing good, it's confusing and you dilute the meaning of the word "good". Remember dogs see in pictures. Most people have a hard time getting their dog to "stay". One of the reasons is because of how they use "good". I'll explain how most people teach 'SIT' and by this point in the book you should be able to point out why it's confusing for the dog.

First the person stands over the dog and says "sit, sit, sit" finally the dog sits and the trainer says "GOOOD" then the dog gets up and gets a treat. Next step is they keep going until the dog gets better and now when it sits the trainer says " good..... goooood" then gives the release word. However, they can't get the dog to stay for more than 15 seconds. This is because the same word they are using to "release" the dog is the same word they are using to tell the dog it is doing good. They now also use the word good for everything. Now over time the word gets diluted, and means less and less also, it means more and more at the same time.

## TO THE DOG "GOOD" MEANS:

- **Be excited**

- **That's correct**

- **Release**

- **Keep sitting**

If you're confused at this point at least you and the dog have something in common. When training dogs, use as few words as possible and make sure you're saying them in a consistent manner. You want to make it as clear as possible for the dog.

## #8 - STAAAYYYYYY

You should not be saying "Staaayyyyyy" to your dog. It's the equivalent of saying "readyyy seeeeeeet GO!" You are amping the dog up, not actually helping. You should also just keep repeating the command that they are doing. If they are sitting, give a reminder with the command "sit" if they are in a 'DOWN' say "down" to keep them in a down. Remember it's not "doowwwwwnnn" it's just "down"

## #9 - GIVING ATTENTION WHILE IN THE KENNEL

This is one that might be the most frustrating and hardest. It is where most people fail in kennel training. The dog pulls at the heart strings of the owner. The dog whines and the owner feels bad. So they go up to the dog's kennel and say things like "you're ok, buddy." Or they yell at the dog to shut up. Let's look at it from the dog's perspective.

Mom puts me in a kennel  - she leaves and I don't want to be in here - I whine and bark - mom walks back in and makes noises that I don't understand (dogs don't speak english incase you forgot) - She leaves - well I didn't get out of the kennel but at least I got attention. - mom walks in again - I start barking and whining - mom lets me out - ohh it must be because I whined and barked. Nice! That's all I have to do and I get out.

By doing this you're making the problem worse. Now obviously If you train with us we will teach the dog "QUIET" and fix it quickly but you can make it easier on yourself by not giving in when you first start. Just ignore the dog while they are barking or whining.

## 10 - NOT HAVING A GAME PLAN AND A GOAL

Everytime you start a training session you should have a goal of where you want to get to. You also should have a game plan of how to get there. I see it too often, where trainers start training a dog and they literally let the dog lead the session. They train reactively instead of proactively. This is about 20% of trainers.

I would say the next level up is trainers who have a goal but not necessarily a game plan to get there. They purely train on how the dog is doing. Which sounds good but there are a couple massive issues with this. First issue, is your system should work on all dogs so you should have a system and game plan. The second, is you train just reactively which is a huge no go. You should be leading the session.

The next is the more diligent trainer. They have a goal and a game plan to get to that goal. However, an issue most have is because they are diligent they get off track worrying about little perfections. They forget the main purpose of the training session because they see the dog not doing a different command perfectly. I'll give an example. A trainer is working "PLACE", they are "HEELING" the dog over to the place spot so they can work it. However the dog keeps messing up on "HEEL" so they stop the whole session to work "HEEL", but the goal of the session was to work "PLACE". Now they have changed a "PLACE" session into a "HEELING" session. If you can fix the issue quick then great! But if it's going to change the course of the session then don't do it. **In short, train proactively not reactively!**

**PAWS,**
for a Fun Fact

Dogs dog to beat the heat. When stuck on an open lawn with little or no shade, unearthing a fresh layer of dirt untouched by sun is a quick way to cool down.

*- MentalFloss.com*

**PAWS**, for a
Notable Quotable

"In a crowded marketplace, fitting in is failing. In a busy marketplace, not standing out is the same as being invisible."

**- SETH GODIN**

*(Seth Godin is an author, entrepreneur and most of all, a teacher. Seth is an entrepreneur, best-selling author, and speaker.)*

# CHAPTER 7

# 10 Virtues Of Dog Training

**JOKE TIME**

*Q: What did one flea say to the other?*
*A: Should we walk or take the dog?*

## #1 - UNDERSTANDING YOUR DOG DOES NOT UNDERSTAND ENGLISH

This is one we see a lot! If you want to communicate well with your dog and be a good dog trainer or owner, you need to understand your dog does not understand what you're saying. Examples:

- **"Fluffy can you sit?"**

- **"It's ok buddy, that dog isn't going to hurt you."**

- **"Fluffy get over here and stop doing that!"**

- **"Be gentle, easy, wait, stayyyyy!"**

As an example: Your dog has no idea what you're saying. Let's use going past another dog on a walk. Your dog typically growls and barks at other dogs when they walk by. You're on a walk and you see a dog in the distance, so you start saying in a sweet voice "hey buddy you're fine it's ok" now you crouch down next to him and start petting him. He has absolutely no idea what you're saying. However, he does know that all the other times he has barked at other dogs you start making those noises. He also knows that you are anxious and can sense your blood pressure rising. Which he knows every time that has happened before, he has been trying to attack another dog. So now instead of calming the dog down like you believe you are, it's like putting gasoline on a fire.

Instead of doing this you need to teach your dog what commands actually mean and teach them to do that. So in this example you would teach 'COME' or 'OFF'. Let's use 'COME' as an example: You would wait until your dog starts pulling or right before it does pull you would say "COME" and bring the dog back to you. You do that over and over so you're changing the dog's picture of the situation. So instead of mom saying sentences the dog doesn't understand and her blood pressure rising, the dog learns "oh when I feel like this mom is going to tell me to come and I'll have to go back to her."

## #2 - UNDERSTANDING THE 4 VARIABLES

**Rule: Only change 1 variable at a time.**

While you are training dogs there are 4 variables you can change. Distance, body language, distraction, and the leash. Remember dogs see in pictures, if you change a variable it could be like changing the whole picture for the dog. So I'll give an example of each while working 'COME':

**Distance** - If you're working 'COME' from 5 feet away, changing to 10 feet away is changing the distance variable.

**Body Language** - when starting 'COME' you want to squat down. Universally, for dogs this is a more inviting position. This is normally the position people are in when they pet them and love them. How you change this picture is by not squatting all the way down or standing up, which changes the body language variable.

**Distraction** - As almost everyone understands when they try to train their own dog for the first time, it listens inside but not outside. Anything that gets the dog's attention off you is changing the variable of distraction.

**Leash** - At the beginning of teaching 'COME', you want to give leash direction towards you with the leash. Not pull, but just tension. As you stop giving tension on the leash, that is changing the leash variable.

## #3 - TAKING A STEP BACK TO GO FORWARD

*Read the previous section on the three variables before reading this.*

The better you get at dog training, the fewer bad reps you should be getting. However, it is inevitable when you are learning or if you are a client, you will get some bad reps. While training, you should think of each training session as a scoreboard on the left side there is 'good reps', on the right side there is 'bad reps'. Each time the dog does something good, the good reps get a point. Each time the dog does something bad, the bad side gets a point. At minimum for each bad rep, you should get 3 good reps. So in each training session it should be 75% good, 25% bad, which is a worse-case scenario. Keep track of that score board in your mind.

What is a good rep? A good rep is if the dog is getting better. No matter what command you're working, the dog is progressing in training. If the answer is not yes then it is a bad rep.

Let's say you are working 'COME' and all of the sudden you start getting multiple bad reps. Good news, and good news. Good news It's your fault as the trainer, not the dog's fault. Good news is that because it's your fault you can fix it. When you start getting bad reps it is typically because you changed more than one variable while training whether you realized it or not. The other option is you are not being as precise with your body language or leash as you should be. Either way, if you start getting bad reps you need to take a step back to make it easier on the dog. You take a step back by reinserting one of the variables you took away or changed.

For example: if you start getting bad reps while working, 'COME'. You just changed from crouching to standing and you tell the dog to "COME" and it seems like the dog has no idea what you were asking it to do. If you get multiple bad reps and you feel the training session is deteriorating, you need to add back in crouching so you can start getting good reps again. Then as they are doing better phase the variable back out.

If you're a newer trainer and you tell me this happened I automatically assume you either moved on too fast and the dog wasn't ready or you changed two variables at once.

As you start getting better you should have to do this less and less. This rule should not exist when you are a GREAT trainer.

## #4 - FAST DOGS GO SLOW, SLOW DOGS GO FAST

Pace with dogs matters a lot. With a dog that does everything super fast while training you need to slow everything down and make it very clear for them. If you try to speed through training with a fast dog they will get more and more frantic. Fast dogs once trained are awesome! However, for most people they are typically the most frustrating to train. That's because for them their brain moves as fast as their body. It is like a kid with ADHD, you must slow everything down and make it clear. If you do this correctly, it will make your training much easier. With fast dogs, you will always be able to speed them back up, but in the mean time slow everything down.

Slow dogs you can go faster with and you should. What I mean by this, is you should constantly be trying to speed the dog up and keep the training fun and exciting. When I say go fast I don't mean in your progression of training, I mean by speeding up how fast you walk and talk. *When in doubt, the fastest way to train a dog is slow.*

## #5 - USING THE LEASH AS A JOYSTICK

When you are training any dog, view the leash as a joystick. Straight up is neutral. From there it is just like a joystick. Forward, left, right, back. The direction you point the leash is the direction you're giving to the dog. This seems obvious but most people aren't conscious of where they are pointing the leash. They will have the dog on their left side, have the leash pointed backwards and with the right hand point for the dog to move forward to a 'PLACE' spot. You can not have off leash training without first having great on leash direction.

## #6 - END EVERY TRAINING SESSION ON A GOOD NOTE

When you end a training session it needs to be on a good "picture". Whatever picture you end on is the picture your dog will start the next training session with. Understand, if you're starting to feel frustrated with the training, your dog probably is as well. If you start getting frustrated, go back a step, make it clear and get a couple good reps. Then give the dog massive praise and give them a bunch of pets and end the training session. This will keep the dogs morale and yours very high. If you keep putting the dog up while it's frustrated it will start to associate training time with being frustrated. Which now you've turned what should be a really fun activity for the dog into a really stressful activity for the dog.

## #7 - NOT TEACHING 'SHAKE', 'SPEAK', OR 'SPIN'

This main reason for this is because these commands are hard to stop from happening once the dog understands them. They are super cute when you first teach them, or when it's convenient. However, once they start doing it nonstop or when it's inconvenient it's not. All three of these commands I never teach my own dogs. I'll give you my reason and you can decide for yourself if you want to teach it or not.

**Shake** - I do a lot of events with my dogs. Like home shows, boat shows, baseball games, football games, hockeys games, etc. At those events my dogs are typically on 'PLACE' spots that are high up. Any dog that knows 'SHAKE' does 'SHAKE' for attention because after they do it they typically get a treat or pets. Because of this I don't want them to 'SHAKE' an older person and cut them with their nails or 'SHAKE' and hit a child in the face.

**Speak** - This one is self explanatory on why you wouldn't want to teach this if you can't shut it off. Typically, trainers teach 'SPEAK' by getting the dog frustrated that they can't have a toy or treat by holding them away from it. Once the dog barks out of frustration, they let the dog go. Then they do it over and over while saying 'SPEAK'. The issue is, now when the dog gets frustrated it thinks to get its way it should bark. Which is what the dog should do because that's what the trainer or owner taught it to do. So when you are giving the dog attention, bark. When you get the toy out and don't give it to them immediately, bark. When it wants to go outside, bark. When you're in public at dinner on a peaceful patio and it wants to get the squirrel but you're holding it back.... Guess what? BARK, BARK, BARK.

**Spin** - This one is admittedly more of a personal one for me. It is just very frustrating when a dog is taught to spin and when it gets the least bit confused it reverts to spinning. Also, when you 'HEEL' the dog and you turn right, but it spins left to go right. Granted the 'HEEL' is fixable but frustrating at first.

## #8 - BEING STRICT WHERE IT MATTERS

When you're training, keep the constant question in your mind "does this matter at this moment?" If you are training the dog to do something new, you want to be aware of what matters and what doesn't. If you're training a dog and they aren't perfect on a past command while you're working the new command does it matter if you fix it? I can't tell you without seeing it. You have to be aware of it yourself. Great trainers understand this well.

General rule: Remember the goal of the session. If you are going to fix something and it's going to be at the expense of the session, Don't do it.

## #9 - WHAT TO LOOK FOR WHEN FINDING A TRAINER

These are my 5 things to look for when looking for a dog trainer.

- **Customer testimonials**
- **Results Oriented**
- **Their dog**
- **See them work with your dog**
- **Guarantee on training**

There are many dog trainers to choose from, and finding the right one for you can be challenging. In the world of dog training, there are no regulations and every trainer certifies themselves. Currently all of my trainers are Make Your Dog Epic Certified. Which, guess what? It means absolutely nothing. The reason being is because there is no governing body over it. There is no one holding us or any dog trainer to a certain standard. When you're looking for dog trainers there are 5 main things I would recommend looking for. I understand while you read this, you're thinking, "He is just saying that because they do all of these things". We are not in every city so we can not reach everyone. My hope is this will help the people we can't personally help find a great trainer near them.

**Customer Testimonials** - This is possibly the most important. You must read and hear what other people are saying about the training. In the world of dog training, every single dog trainer certifies themselves and claims to be the best. Because of this, you MUST read reviews from past customers. Read with discernment on reviews. Every single business gets bad reviews. You can not please everyone. If you see bad reviews, ask yourself if you would've been mad about that as well. Also, see how the business responded. Did they try to fix the issue or blame the customer? Whatever they did to them there is a high possibility they will do to you.

**Results Oriented** - In the dog training world so many trainers and customers are focused on the number of lessons. This should not be the focus, the focus should be results! If your dog does 100 lessons but still doesn't listen, what's the point? If the dog does 2 lessons, and does everything you want the dog to be able to do that's more important. You do not want someone selling you an amount of time, you want results.

**Their Dog** - You want to see the trainer's dog. This is very important. Think about it, if their dog won't listen will they be able to get yours to listen? Typically, when you see a trainer's dog you are seeing the best they can possibly do. If possible, you also want to see the dog in a public place not just where they train. If they only show you their dog at a training facility it's probably because they don't listen around distractions. If they show off their dog to you and you're impressed, and would be thrilled if your dog did that then it's a great sign. A trainer's dog is kind-of like their resume or diploma of sorts. Showing they know what they are talking about.

**See Them Work with Your Dog** - This is possibly the most important. You need to see that they don't just speak a good game, they can actually show you. The trainer needs to be able to show you some demonstration of their training skills before you sign up. Seeing their dog is fine. But more importantly you need to see them train your specific dog. Make sure that their training methods are right for you.

**Guarantee on Training** - Do they offer a money back guarantee on training? If not, what guarantee of training? Too many trainers operate under the "you get what you get and don't throw a fit" method. The other option is the "it might stick" method. Basically, what that means is the training might "stick" so there is a chance after the training is over that the training doesn't work. Ask about guarantees on training, and you want to see if they are dodging the question or not.

Hopefully this helps you in your journey of finding a great dog trainer. We don't care who you train with as long as the end result is happy dogs and happy customers.

## #10 - KEEP IT SIMPLE STUPID

When I was in the military, they loved using acronyms, and one of their favorites was KISS: Keep It Simple, Stupid. It's widely used, and it applies to dog training in every aspect. You need to keep every aspect of training simple, for both the dog and the owners. If it's too complicated for the dog, it'll take longer for them to understand. Likewise, if you make it complicated, the owner will struggle to get the dog to listen.

We offer our first lesson for just 50 cents, so owners can try it before committing. We get to tell them more about us. It's also a chance for us to learn about their dog and their goals because every dog is different, and everyone's goals are different.

To keep this short, a trainer had come out before for about five private lessons where they worked with the dog and client simultaneously. However, the mom recently called us because the behaviors were still happening. The dog was a 170-pound Great Dane, pulling so hard it would literally drag her down and then down the street. The only person in the house who could still take the dog on a walk was dad. I asked about the previous training, wanting to know what went wrong and what went well.

> **"...CLIENTS DON'T WANT TO BECOME EXPERT DOG TRAINERS. THEY DON'T WANT TO INVEST THE MANY HOURS IT TOOK FOR YOU TO LEARN YOUR METHODS. THEY'RE PAYING YOU TO TRAIN THEIR DOG..."**

The trainer had them using a prong collar, treats, and an e-collar all at the same time, which I understand is common for some trainers. The issue is that you shouldn't have to be a skilled handler to have a dog that listens. If someone is paying you to train them and their dog, the client shouldn't have to possess expert handling skills. Your training method should be so simple that even a typical six-year-old could get the dog to listen.

As a trainer, you have to understand that clients don't want to become expert dog trainers. They don't want to invest the many hours It took for you to learn your methods. They're paying you to train their dog and get it to listen to them. If you make it too complicated, nobody will be able to replicate your system, and you're doing them and their family a disservice. With every dog you train, you should imagine they'll need to listen to a 90-year-old grandma who can't raise her voice or be physical with the dog.

**PAWS**, for a
Notable Quotable

"Practice does not make perfect. Only perfect practice makes perfect."

**- VINCE LOMBARDI**

*(A man recognized as one of the greatest coaches in American football history.)*

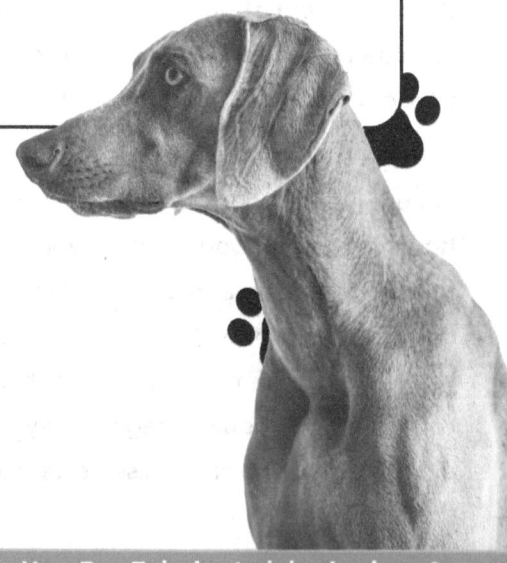

# CHAPTER 8

# Anxiety and Aggression

**JOKE TIME**

*Q: What did the dog say to the sandpaper?*
*A: Ruff!*

*Before reading this, read the first chapter "Dogs See In Pictures".*

This could be a whole book in itself. Instead of getting into the behaviorist side of things, trying to understand why the dog is doing something, I'm going to explain to you how we use training to fix and manage these behaviors. We are going to assume you have trained with us and now your dog understands and listens to commands. Now the next step, is behavior modification using those commands.

> **NOTE: IF THE DOG DOESN'T UNDERSTAND THE COMMANDS AND IS DOING THEM FOR THE FIRST TIME THEN THE BELOW WILL NOT WORK.**

The commands are going to be a tool that stops the bad behavior instantly, but the goal is to reshape the dog's picture of the situation. We are going to pick back up on the situation of the first chapter of going on a walk and your dog barks, growls or lunges at other dogs. When this is happening it is not necessary to understand what your dog is thinking. What I mean by this is the solution is still the same, it doesn't matter the underlying cause. If your dog is thinking "I need to protect mom" or "I want to play" or "I want to fight that dog" the solution is the same. We need to use the command "OFF" and or "COME". "OFF" means move away physically and mentally, but not that you are in trouble. This is key! We don't want your dog thinking you're mad or this other dog is bad, just "I need to move away".

Your dog starts barking and we say "OFF". The dog stops barking and turns away. You can be as strict or lenient as you want with this. One of our trainers can help you through it as well. Some dogs are so triggered or have been through so much trauma that they lose all privileges when it comes to other dogs. Sometimes even looking at the dog we tell them "OFF" so they aren't allowed to look. You will know your dog well. The moment you see your dog start working itself up you should say "OFF".

The result of doing this over and over is the dog's picture starts to get reshaped and the trigger disappears. The old picture was, "I see a dog I start barking and growling and I think I'm doing a good job because mom is saying things I don't understand". The new picture is "I see a dog. Mom is going to tell me to move away if I start barking, might as well not do it". Or the perfect reshaping of the picture is "I see a dog and now I'm no longer anxious or aggressive at all so I can play with them".

The reason we offer our first lesson for 50 cents is so we can see your dog and hear your story and give you realistic expectations of where we can help you and your dog. We have had situations where people have almost given up hope and surrendered dogs, and we are able to come to that first lesson and completely change their life. This absolutely thrills us! Our whole goal is to give more freedom through dog training.

**PAWS,**
for a Pro Tip

When dealing with people who break agreements and go against their word in order to maximize their profits, **RUN**!

**PAWS**, for a
Notable Quotable

# "Drifting, without aim or purpose, is the first cause of failure."

## - NAPOLEON HILL
*(Best-selling author of Think & Grow Rich.)*

# CHAPTER 9

# Dog Quiz

**JOKE TIME**

*Q: What do a dog and a cellphone have in common?*

*A: Both have collar ID!*

This is a fun quiz you can do by yourself or challenge your family with! It will get harder as it goes on. Select the correct breed.

A · **Labrador retriever**
B · **Chow Chow**
C · **German Shepherd**
D · **Seberian Husky**

**Golden Retriever · A**
**Bulldog · B**
**Border Collie · C**
**Australian Cattle dog · D**

A · **Labrador retriever**
B · **Chow Chow**
C · **German Shepherd**
D · **Seberian Husky**

Chow Chow · A

German Shepherd · B

Beagle · C

Akita · D

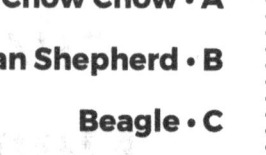

A · Belgian Malinois

B · French Bulldog

C · Australian Shepherd

D · Tibetan Mastiff

Australian Shepherd · A

Bedlington Terrier · B

Border Collie · C

Belgian Malinois · D

A · German Shepherd

B · Bull Terrier

C · Bedlington Terrier

D · Belgian Malinois

**Chow Chow · A**
**Tibetan Mastiff · B**
**Akita · C**
**Irish wolfhound · D**

**A · Akita**
**B · Irish wolfhound**
**C · Chow Chow**
**D · Tibetan Mastiff**

**Basset Hound · A**
**Neapolitan Mastiff · B**
**Shar Pei · C**
**Chinese crested · D**

**A · Chinese crested**
**B · Tibetan Mastiff**
**C · Neapolitan Mastiff**
**D · Rottweiler**

Irish wolfhound · A

Brussels Griffon · B

Neapolitan Mastiff · C

Komondor · D

A · Shar Pei

B · Neapolitan Mastiff

C · Brussels Griffon

D · Chinese crested

German Shepherd · A

Seberian Husky · B

Shar Pei · C

Labrador Retriever · D

A · Tibetan Mastiff

B · Neapolitan Mastiff

C · Borzoi

D · Bull Terrier

Bedlington Terrier • A

Border Collie • B

Pig • C

Belgian Malinois • D

A • Prairie dog

B • Field Dog

C • Mountain Dog

D • Water Dog

Portuguese Mountain Dog • A

Portuguese Field Dog • B

Portuguese Prairie Dog • C

Portuguese Water Dog • D

**PAWS,**
for a Fun Fact

Dogs dream when
they sleep.

*- MentalFloss.com*

## Correct Answers

| | | |
|---|---|---|
| 1. D | 7. D | 13. D |
| 2. A | 8. A | 14. C |
| 3. C | 9. A | 15. B |
| 4. C | 10. A | 16. C |
| 5. B | 11. B | 17. A |
| 6. A | 12. A | 18. D |

**PAWS**, for a
Notable Quotable

"Before success comes in any man's life, he is sure to meet with much temporary defeat, and, perhaps, some failure. When defeat overtakes a man, the easiest and most logical thing to do is to quit. That is exactly what the majority of men do. More than five hundred of the most successful men this country has ever known told the author their greatest success came just one step beyond the point at which defeat had overtaken them."

### - NAPOLEON HILL

*(Bestselling self-help author and the former apprentice of the world's wealthiest man, Andrew Carnegie.)*

**Section Two**

# The Business of Dog Training

**PAWS**, for a
Notable Quotable

"It takes a lot of hard work to make
something simple, to truly understand the
underlying challenges and come up with
elegant solutions. Simplicity is the ultimate
sophistication...That's been one of my
mantras – focus and simplicity. Simple can be
harder than complex: You have to work hard
to get your thinking clean to make it simple.
But it's worth it in the end because once you
get there, you can move mountains."

**- STEVE JOBS**

*(The co-founder of Apple, the founder of
NeXT, and the former CEO of PIXAR.)*

# CHAPTER 11

# The Power of the Weekly Meeting

**(DEPENDABILITY IS THE MOST IMPORTANT ABILITY)**

At Make Your Dog Epic, we schedule a weekly, one-hour, recurring meeting where we look at big wins of the week, the status of our team's key performance indicators, any big issues or burning fires that need to be resolved, following up on the status of action items from last week, assigning action items for the following week, and situational dog training.

## The items we typically cover in our weekly meeting include:

- » Big wins of the week
- » The vision of Make Your Life Epic Dog Training
- » The status of our key performance indicators (quantifiable numbers and key performance metrics)
- » Burning fires
- » Follow-up action items (did everyone get their assignments done?)
- » Assign action items (who, what, when, where, why?)

Our commitment to follow this agenda each week will keep our company from ever drifting too far away from our core customers, our core vision, our core brand and our core values.

**PAWS**, for a
Notable Quotable

"The time that leads to mastery is
dependent on the intensity of our focus."

**- ROBERT GREENE**

*(Best-selling author of Mastery, The 50th Law, The Law of
Human Nature & The 48 Laws of Power.)*

# CHAPTER 12

# Tracking

**(WHY WE MUST MEASURE WHAT WE TREASURE)**

We track multiple metrics every single week. It's vital for the business and customer satisfaction, that we track our daily and weekly key performance indicators.

## A few of the weekly metrics we track are:

1. Leads
2. Where leads are coming from - (advertising sources, word of mouth, etc)
3. Leads booked
4. Leads sold
5. How much cash we received
6. How much we did in sales
7. How much we are spending on advertising
8. Cost per click with advertising
9. How many objective Google reviews we received
10. How many video testimonials we received
11. How long its taking employees to train dogs
12. How much each dog is progressing per day
13. Tracking how long it takes for our boarding school packages to be properly trained
14. Tracking how long it take for each trainer to train dogs
15. Etc.

By holding our team accountable for tracking our daily key performance indicators, we can keep our finger on the pulse of the business without having to be there with each member of our team. Holding them accountable during every moment of their work day. As an owner, there are many things that go on during your day to day. You can not hold the hand of every employee at all times. So you must have the systems and processes in place while tracking all key performance indicators to hold them accountable.

**PAWS**, for a
Notable Quotable

"Measure what you treasure. What you track won't be allowed to slack."

**- CLAY CLARK**

*(Former Oklahoma Young U.S. SBA Entrepreneur of the Year.)*

# CHAPTER 13

# Don't Reinvent the Wheel

**(FOLLOW THE PROVEN PROCESSES
& SUCCESS SYSTEMS)**

As an owner of a Make Your Dog Epic licensed business, I would highly recommend that you follow the proven, turn-key, and best-practice systems that I have developed. However, because you are a licensee and not a franchisee, I cannot demand that you do.

However, as a client of one of our locations, and seeing as you pay us and not the other way around, my hope is that we can WOW you so you can see the value of implementing our proven systems and processes.

I know as a dog owning consumer, you are constantly bombarded with social media videos, self-proclaimed dog training experts, and your mother-in-law, all telling you how you should train your dog. However, when you invest in us, we are committed to wowing you so you are happy to tell your family and friends about the quality of the results that we delivered.

To the dog trainers: I would highly recommend that you follow best-practice systems, as opposed to guessing, hoping and wishing through the process of entropy, success will magically appear. Your goal is to create happy customers and happy dogs.

To Make Your Dog Epic location owners: we have made this business and the dog training ownership as empowering, simple, and as easy as possible by supporting you as a trainer.

**PAWS**, for a
Notable Quotable

"The size of your success is measured by the strength of your desire; the size of your dream; and how you handle disappointment along the way."

**- ROBERT KIYOSAKI**

*(The best-selling author of the Rich Dad Poor Dad book series, the host of the Rich Dad Radio Show and a man who has sold over 45 million copies of his self-help books, and a guest on Clay Clark's ThrivetimeShow.)*

# CHAPTER 14

# The Group Interview

**(WHY NOTHING WILL WORK, IF WE WON'T)**

As an owner, hiring can be one of the most frustrating things. I'm busy and you're busy, but you and I must block off time to conduct weekly interviews to find people who will best represent your company. I love scheduling group interviews because it saves time, and allows me to see how candidates compare with each other in a literal side-by-side comparison (A tryout of sorts). If you don't want to do group interviews, then you are going to have to block out many hours throughout your week to interview potential candidates who might or might not show up on time or at all for their interviews. Because I realize that 40% of potential candidates don't have the mental capacity or the diligence needed to actually show up on time for their initial interviews, I love the group interview format. When someone responds to a job post, our team schedules them for an interview.

## "75% of employees steal from the workplace and most do so repeatedly." - U.S. Department of Commerce.

https://www.forbes.com/sites/ivywalker/2018/12/28/your-employees-are-probably-stealing-from-you-here-are-five-ways-to-put-an-end-to-it/?sh=42cda3863386

## "32% of employees are engaged in the workplace." - Gallup

https://www.shrm.org/resourcesandtools/hr-topics/behavioral-competencies/global-and-cultural-effectiveness/pages/new-gallup-poll-employee-disengagement-hits-9-year-high.aspx

During an interview, many business owners spend massive quantities of time going on and on, about their company and their vision while the candidates sit quietly, scanning the room for a blunt object with which they can respectfully bash in their skull to stop the boredom. Candidates begin to feel as though the person interviewing them has no gameplan or agenda, because they don't. To make matters worse, most companies delegate the recruitment and interviewing process to "the new guy" or the person on your staff who hasn't quite found his place within your company culture. This is terrible. My friend, the person conducting the interviews must look sharp and must be a confidence-inspiring powerhouse who can follow the perfect interview agenda every time which includes:

- Clarifying the goals of the company
- Clarifying the goals of the candidate
- Clarifying the expectations of the job
- Clarify the compensation of the job
- Clarifying the career path of the job
- Answering any questions
- Clarifying the next steps for the applicants

## When hiring you are looking for the 4 E's

» Energy – Does the candidate have the energy to bring enthusiasm to the workplace every day?

» Energize – Does the candidate have the ability to energize those around him or her?

» Edge – Does the candidate have the edge needed to make the tough decisions?

» Execute – Does the candidate have the ability to execute and actually get their job done?

» BONUS – I have also found that it is extremely important that you search for candidates who are coachable.

*"ENTREPRENEURS SOLVE THE WORLD'S PROBLEMS
AND UNAPOLOGETICALLY MAKE MONEY DOING IT."
— CLAY CLARK*

**"Don't be an ASK Hole."**

# Ask·hole [ask-hole]

*noun*

1. A person who asks questions, yet doesn't want to know the answers.
2. A person who chooses to not have the mental capacity and tenacity needed to implement proven systems.
3. A person who refuses to bore down and do the work because they struggle with perpetual boredom.

**PAWS**, for a
Notable Quotable

"Mediocre people suffer
from boredom while the
greats bore down."

- **CLAY CLARK**

☆ ☆ ☆ ☆ ☆

# CHAPTER 15

# Gather Objective Google Reviews from Happy Clients

**(WHY YOUR ONLINE REPUTATION DETERMINES THE
AMOUNT OF YOUR COMPENSATION)**

As I said earlier, there is no governing body over dog training. So, what people say about you and how good of a job you do really does matter. Gathering objective reviews from your current & past customers is one of the most important things you could do in any business, not to mention an industry that relies on Google reviews as the only way to show you did a good job. In fact, around the year 2017 I had the opportunity to work with a couple whose business was stuck every year at approximately $400,000 per year of annual revenue. However, within just one short year we helped them to grow from $400,000 to $598,000 in annual revenue. In fact, this couple I was working with was actually resorting to buying fake awards when I first met them, in order to convince their customers of their legitimacy which is ironic. When meeting a potential client, bring your own dogs to show people what you can do. Your past customers are the only thing that can truly show people what you can do.

You cannot afford to sit back and wait for objective Google reviews to flow in and to come to you. Go get those reviews from your real customers. Once you have the most objective Google reviews from your current and former clients you will climb to the top of Google search results quickly. Most business owners fail here by passively waiting for their customers to provide them with reviews and acting as though the negative reviews that have been written don't impact the buying decisions of potential customers. In this world of anonymous reviews, the trolls can quickly gain control, so you must proactively e-mail, call, and ask your happy customers to write a review for you. Competitors, former employees, and people you decided not to hire will actually invest the time needed to give you bad reviews.

Most sane people will not typically go out of their way to request reviews. If you are not proactive about asking for reviews from your happy customers, you will wake up one morning and discover you have four negative reviews and no positive reviews.

Years ago, I worked with a couple of clients who would always talked about how God was going to bless them because they were believers in Jesus and the prosperity mindset.

However, these two clients refused to get more than 3-5 objective reviews per week from their real customers.

After investing a copious amount of time with those two clients I was able to finally convince them, although God wanted to bless them, in order for them to get to the top of the Google search engine algorithm, they would need to gather the most Google reviews in their service area. As a result of embracing implementing this concept and many other proven, best-practice systems, this super-appreciative client was able to grow their stagnant business from 1 location to 15+ locations.

**PAWS**, for a
Notable Quotable

## "Sucess is a choice."

### - NAPOLEON HILL

*(Bestselling self-help author and the former apprentice of
the world's wealthiest man, Andrew Carnegie.)*

**PAWS**,
for a Pro Tip

Nefarious people tend to
communicate passive-
aggressively via email and
text while avoiding talking
over the phone or face-to-face
meetings at all costs.

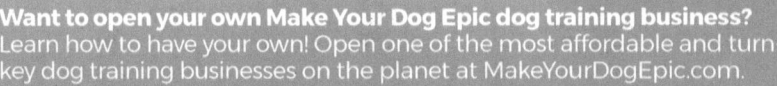

**PAWS**, for a
Notable Quotable

"If you pick the right people and give them
the opportunity to spread their wings and
put compensation as a career behind it
you almost don't have to manage them."

## - JACK WELCH

*(The former CEO who grew GE by 4,000%
during his tenure at GE.)*

**BUSINESS TIP!**

# CHAPTER 16

# Gather Video Reviews from Happy Clients

## (WHY REAL HUMANS ON THE REAL PLANET EARTH MUST ACTUALLY ENDORSE THE SERVICE WE PROVIDE)

People need to see video testimonials from your real customers that you are actually working with. I cannot say it enough how valuable getting video reviews from your real customers is! If you're reading this as a client and you own a business, immediately go out and get 100 Google reviews and 100 video reviews from your happy customers and post them everywhere. People need to see your customers are SUPER happy about the services you have provided.

*A note for our trainers and owners: if you do not feel like your customer would say good things on a Google review or a video review you yourself did something wrong. Customers should be ecstatic after training with you. You should've just changed their life! The difference between a well-trained dog and an untrained dog can be someone's sanity!*

**Want to open your own Make Your Dog Epic dog training business?** Learn how to have your own! Open one of the most affordable and turn-key dog training businesses on the planet at MakeYourDogEpic.com.

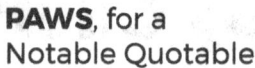

**PAWS**, for a
Notable Quotable

"The Tiffany Theory states that a gift delivered in a box from Tiffany's will have a higher perceived value than one in no box or a plain box. That's not because the recipient is a fool; it's because in our society, we gift-wrap everything: our politicians, our corporate heads, our movie and TV stars, and even our toilet paper. Public Relations is like gift wrapping."

**- MICHAEL LEVINE**

*(Best-selling author and the PR consultant of choice for Michael Jackson, Pizza Hut, Nike, Prince, and a multiple-time guest on the ThrivetimeShow podcast.)*

# CHAPTER 17

# Never-Stop Advertising

## (WITHOUT LEADS YOUR BUSINESS WILL BLEED)

If you are the top dog trainer in the world and do a better job than anyone in the history of dog training, that's great. But it does not matter at all if you do not have leads. That is exactly why we choose to throw our brand name behind passionate trainers like you! We want to magnify great dog trainers. It does not matter if you are a good salesperson, if you don't have leads. It does not matter If you have motivational quotes all over your facility if you do not have leads. It is very simple: your business bleeds if you do not have leads. In a perfect world, you wouldn't have to spend money on marketing to new customers and word of mouth would organically make your business grow exponentially forever.

The reality, however, whether you are Nike, McDonald's, Southwest Airlines, or Disney World, you are going to have to invest in consistent advertising to stay in the minds of your ideal and likely buyers. The big question is this: how much money does it cost your company to attract one customer? This is where a tracking program comes in. You want to track your leads. Where are your leads coming from? How many leads are you getting per week?

### PAWS, for a Notable Quotable

"Before success comes in any man's life, he is sure to meet with much temporary defeat, and, perhaps, some failure. When defeat overtakes a man, the easiest and most logical thing to do is to quit. That is exactly what the majority of men do. More than five hundred of the most successful men this country has ever known told the author their greatest success came just one step beyond the point at which defeat had overtaken them."

**- NAPOLEON HILL**

*(The best-selling author of Think & Grow Rich.)*

# CHAPTER 18
# Dog Math

## How long does it take to train your dog?

Most wonderful people like you, who allow us to train their dog, want to know how long the proper training of your dog is going to take? And that is a valid question that I will attempt to answer with the following DOG MATH equations:

## Dog Training Time Required

Example Packages:

- 🐾 The Basic Package = Typically 1 Week of Training
- 🐾 The Advanced Package = Typically 2 Weeks of Training
- 🐾 The Epic Package = Typically 3 Weeks of Training

**PAWS**, for a Notable Quotable

"Running a successful business requires Three P's: Planning, Procedures & Policies."

**- CHET HOLMES**

*(The best-selling author of The Ultimate Sales Machine and a legendary business growth consultant before the time of his death.)*

Whether we are talking about training dogs or teaching humans to speak Spanish, everyone learns at a different pace. However, once we are confident that your dog has been well-trained we offer on-going and perpetual training for the rest of your dog's life so that you, as an owner, and they as the dog, can get additional training and tune ups on dog skills on a weekly basis.

### How long does it take to train your employees and local owners to become dog trainers?

If you are familiar with dogs and are a very physically coordinated individual, we believe that it will take you approximately 4 weeks of on-site training to learn how to become a dog trainer depending where you receive your training from. However, if you already skilled at training dogs it may be much faster. The following skills will be helpful to you as a location owner:

- How a Workflow Works
- How to Properly Train Dogs
- How to Train Dog Trainers
- How to Conduct Weekly Group Job Interviews
- How to Conduct Your Weekly Staff Meeting
- How to Conduct Your Daily Staff Huddles
- How to Manage Your Time And Block Out Your Calendar Effectively
- How to Manage Your Team (Master the Art of Follow-up)
- How to On-Board New Employees
- How to Fire Employees That Refuse to Follow Your Dog Training Systems
- How to Optimize Your Local Internet Presence
- How to Optimize Your Local Google Map
- How Online Reputation Works
- How Online Advertising Works
- How to Track Your Weekly Numbers
- How to Sell In the Win-Win Manner That We Recommend (we do not believe in using high-pressure sales techniques, and not using various manipulative sales strategies)

If you are interested in becoming a Make Your Dog Epic business owner, we would love to speak with you. We are currently the most affordable dog training business opportunity on the planet. To schedule a free consultation, simply find the "Want to Open a Make Your Dog Epic Business/Location?" button which is found under the "Locations" button on the website. You can also simply fill out the "CONTACT" button which is found on our website at: https://MakeYourDogEpic.com/Contact/

 **PAWS**, for a
Notable Quotable

"The secret of happiness is minimizing the amount of time you spend with people you don't choose to be with. This is just math!"

**- PHIL LIBIN**

*(The Co-founder of Evernote.)*

 **PAWS**,
for a Pro Tip

If someone pushes you out of a business relationship under the guise that you are doing a bad job, but then asks you to sign a non-compete, you are not doing a bad job. Instead, you have made them feel inferior and self conscious.

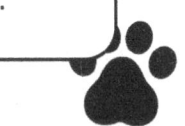

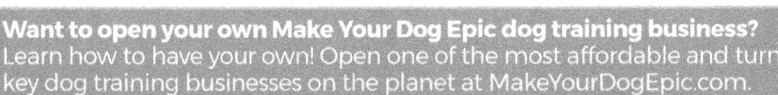

**PAWS**, for a
Notable Quotable

"I realized that becoming a master of karate was not about learning 4,000 moves but about doing just a handful of moves 4,000 times."

## - CHET HOLMES

*(The best-selling author of The Ultimate Sales Machine and a legendary business growth consultant before the time of his death.)*

CHAPTER 19

*BUSINESS TIP!*

# The Path to Promotion & Being the Perfect Employee

The path to promotion at Make Your Dog Epic Dog Training is not complicated, yet it does require hard work and diligence (the consistent application of effort).

**Dependability** - Dependability is the number one ability that we look for in the employees that we hire and promote into key leadership positions. As of the time that I am writing this, I have been self-employed for 28 consecutive years and I have never taken a "sick day." I have never ghosted my employer because it's my birthday, and I don't take off the Monday, Tuesday and Wednesday before Thanksgiving and the week of Christmas. Why? Because nothing works unless I do and we do. When a customer decides to entrust us with the training of their dog we must deliver results. Because if we do not WOW our customers, they can simply fire us by taking their hard-earned money somewhere else.

**PAWS**, for a Notable Quotable

"You cannot control what happens to you, but you can control your attitude toward what happens to you, and in that, you will be mastering change rather than allowing it to master you."

**- BRIAN TRACY**
*(Legendary self-help author, business trainer, business mentor and business growth consultant.)*

**Energy** - If you decide to own a Make Your Dog Epic Dog Training location, know you need to bring great energy every day, not weird energy. As of the time I am writing this, I went to bed last night at 9 PM and I woke up today at 3 AM. Why? That is my routine and that is how I have created the time needed to create several successful organizations while helping to raise 5 incredible kids, 4 goats, dozens of chickens, 11 cats and 1 dog (by the name of "Davis"). You need to do whatever you need to do before you get to work every day to bring GREAT ENERGY, CONTAGIOUS ENERGY and POSITIVE ENERGY to the workplace. No moping, no yawning, and no slacking. You must bring great ENERGY every day.

**Energize** - You must work to energize the dogs you are training and the people we are working with. It's your job to help create

**PAWS**, for a
Notable Quotable

"Render more service than you are paid for and eventually you will be paid more for less services rendered."

**- NAPOLEON HILL**

*(The best-selling self-help author of all-time whose books have been constantly quoted by the world's most successful people.)*

an environment of enthusiasm, and if the person next to you is moping it's your job to pull the weeds of negativity and to sew the seeds of positivity immediately. You don't want to promote someone to a management position who does not have the ability to energize themselves and others.

**Execute** -  You must learn how to effectively train dogs and you must carry a to-do-list and clipboard at all times if you want to be successful. It's very difficult to follow a checklist or remember what tasks you are supposed to do if you do not have them easily accessible and in front of you at all times. The pen is for

**PAWS**, for a
Notable Quotable

"If you pick the right people and give them the opportunity to spread their wings, and put compensation as a carrier behind it you almost don't have to manage them."

**- JACK WELCH**
*(The former CEO of GE who grew the company by 4,000% during his tenure.)*

remembering and the mind is for thinking. We can never become so busy that we forget to execute proven processes and best-practice systems. If you have the best attitude in the world, it will not matter if you cannot train dogs or do your job effectively. Our company has been designed to be repeatable by our locations and clients, which is why our service is one of the most affordable services in the nation. However, our systems quickly become unrepeatable and unaffordable if everyone is not implementing best-practice systems.

**Edge** - You must be able to make the tough call and to do hard things. When you walk by a piece of trash at the office and no one else is around, do you pick it up? When you catch another employee engaging in a nefarious activity, will you let your manager know? Having been self-employed and having mentored literally thousands of business owners, I can tell you patterns that I often see in cowardly, weak and feeble-minded people. Weak people love to become keyboard warriors and type things that they would never say to your face. Weak people love to embezzle money (embezzlement takes place when a person intentionally uses funds for a different purpose that they were intended to be used for, such as taking money from their business partner to enrich themselves, paying themselves $80,000+ to market their services to themselves, dramatically reducing the amount of money they are paying their

**PAWS**, for a
Notable Quotable

"Good checklists, on the other hand, are precise. They are efficient, to the point, and easy to use even in the most difficult situations. They do not try to spell out everything—a checklist cannot fly a plane. Instead, they provide reminders of only the most critical and important steps— the ones that even the highly skilled professionals using them could miss. Good checklists are, above all, practical."

**- ATUL GAWANDE**

*(Best-selling author of Checklist Manifesto and an American surgeon, writer and public speaker. He also has worked at the Harvard Medical School as their Professor of Surgery.)*

partner without discussing it first and without having the legal authority to do so). Weak people love to avoid eye contact and prefer to communicate via text message and email. Weak people love to do the wrong thing in a quiet way for their own financial benefit. When you work at Make Your Dog Epic you must do unto others as you would have them do unto you.

**Passion** - You must have a passion for life and it must show up in the workplace and in all you do. If you want to become a Make Your Dog Epic Dog Training business owner YOU CAN DO IT! All you have to do is prove yourself as the best employee and teammate you can possibly be and you are on the path to success.

"Therefore all things whatsoever ye would that men should do to you, do ye even so to them: for this is the law and the prophets."

**- MATTHEW 7:12**
*(From The Bible.)*

## What Does One Need to Do to Become Promoted At Make Your Dog Epic Dog Training?

🐾 **Step 1** - Show up to work on time and early every day.

🐾 **Step 2** - Beat your boss to work every day (if you want to get promoted really quickly)

🐾 **Step 3** - Work accurately throughout the day while bringing positive energy and being honest.

🐾 **Step 4** - Don't leave work until the job is done.

**PAWS,**
for a Fun Fact

Dalmatians don't have spots when they are born.

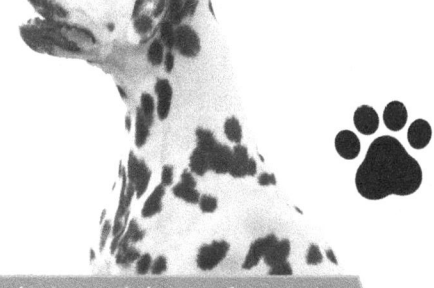

**PAWS**, for a
Notable Quotable

"REMEMBERING THAT YOU ARE
GOING TO DIE IS THE BEST WAY
I KNOW TO AVOID THE TRAP OF
THINKING YOU HAVE SOMETHING
TO LOSE. YOU ARE ALREADY NA-
KED. THERE IS NO REASON NOT TO
FOLLOW YOUR HEART."

- STEVE JOBS

*(The co-founder of Apple, the founder of NeXT
and the former CEO of PIXAR.)*

# CHAPTER 20

# Do you want to Own a Make Your Dog Epic Location?

**(A SPECIAL MESSAGE FROM CLAY CLARK)**

Are you looking for a business vehicle that you can start quickly and requires minimal startup cost? Are you looking to earn extra income? Have you ever thought of opening your own business? Have you ever thought of opening a business, but you couldn't quite figure out the right business niche, products and services to offer? Are you tired of working in politically correct corporate America? If you earned both time and financial freedom, what would you do with your extra time and income? If you are interested in a Make Your Dog Epic location ownership, reach out to us at www.MakeYourDogEpic.com/contact.

Having grown up without money and in a family where my father was delivering pizzas and working the night shift at a gas station to make ends meet in his late thirties to provide for our family despite having a college degree, I know what it's like to start with nothing and to build a successful, scalable and turn-key business model. I started my first business out of my parent's Cokato, Minnesota basement at the age of 15, (www.DJConnection.com). I know what it's like to work at three jobs simultaneously (Applebee's, Target & DirecTV) in order to save up enough money to get my entertainment business and bridal expo / wedding show business off the ground.

I know what it is like to actually work 119 hours per week (which is 17 Hours per day) in order to build a successful business that is capable of producing both financial and time freedom for me and my family. I love entrepreneurship! I love finding a problem, solving it, creating a win-win price point for businesses and customers and scaling it and that is a big reason why I love dog training!!! I love creating jobs for wonderful people like you to transform their dog from a terrorist into their best friend and I love creating jobs for our wonderful employees who love to deliver their training skills with a spirit of excellence.

Since the age of 15, I have not stopped starting, growing and scaling successful businesses because I enjoy it, I'm good at it and it is what I have learned how to master in these last 29 years of being self-employed. Around the age of 25, after I had started and grown several successful companies including: www.DJConnection.com, The Tulsa Wedding Show, a videography company (which was known as Cherished Traditions Videography at the time), I began to receive more and more businesses awards, and it occurred to me that I should write some business / self-help books to document my proven processes and business growth systems.

After writing those books, MASSIVE companies like UPS, Hewlett Packard, O'Reilly Auto Parts, QuikTrip, Boeing, Bama Companies and colleges kept asking me to educate, to inspire and to teach their groups how to start and grow a successful business. However, after delivering well over 300 keynote presentations, I discovered that audiences enjoyed my training and workshops. Yet they found it to be impossible to really learn how to build successful business systems and scalable businesses without on-going weekly mentorship, training and accountability.

Having helped thousands of entrepreneurs to turn their business ideas into successful companies, I've discovered teaching someone to grow successful companies requires on-going weekly mentorship and accountability so you don't begin to lose focus and drift over time. That is why I started coaching clients on a weekly and on-going basis. The results we have been able to produce for our clients has been life-changing for them (and you can watch thousands of real-life client success stories at www.ThrivetimeShow.com).

If you decide to join the Make Your Dog Epic family, you will have the opportunity for my team and I to essentially mentor you, coach you, and hold you accountable on a weekly basis. We want your business to Thrive.

**PAWS**, for a
Notable Quotable

## "The time will never be just right, you must act now."

### - NAPOLEON HILL

*(The best-selling author of Think & Grow Rich, the book that changed my life. Napoleon Hill's writings had such a huge impact on me that I actually named my son Aubrey Napoleon-Hill Clark after Napoleon Hill in honor of the positive and life-changing impact that his writings had on my life.)*

I host multiple MIND-BLOWING, INTERACTIVE and ENGAGING TWO-DAY business growth conferences you can attend for free as a member of the Make Your Dog Epic team. I am passionate about making sure each and every location we support does well. I sincerely want you to thrive because I earn revenue for helping you, mentoring you, guiding you down the path, and assisting with online advertising. We offer each and every location with the weekly business growth coaching, consulting, mentoring and accountability, to ensure nobody drifts to success. It is up to you how much of our assets you take advantage of.

## HOW MUCH DOES IT COST TO OPEN A MAKE YOUR DOG EPIC DOG TRAINING BUSINESS?

- 🐾 You must have a dog that will serve as your best friend and demonstration dog for customers.

- 🐾 You must have a vehicle to safely transport dogs.

- 🐾 You must supply a safe and climate controlled location for the training of dogs.

- 🐾 You must use a dog training technique that utilizes industry best-practices and includes positive reinforcement that we refer to as: focus-based, positive reinforcement training and methodology.

- 🐾 We include a program for the weekly on-going mentorship, training, coaching, online advertisement management, website maintenance, search engine optimization, etc. for you to access at your will.

- 🐾 You pay 6% of your gross revenue, plus a 750/month flat fee that includes the use of our brand name and logo for you to utilize on products or marketing materials.

🐾 You receive a branded local page on our website, a phone number for initial client calls, and an opportunity to utilize our mentorship and business knowledge as much or as little as you like. You set prices, packages, control on-going appointments, and control employee wages.

🐾 We require you to use whatever best-practice training techniques you are most comfortable with, and have produced great results for you while training dogs. We only require you to incorporate positive reinforcement training into your routine. We do not consider the use of shock collars as a best-practice training technique. Some trainers prefer the use of e-collars while others use clicker training and others positive reinforcement only. That is up to you.

## WHAT WILL YOUR WEEKLY SCHEDULE LOOK LIKE AS A MAKE YOUR DOG EPIC BUSINESS OWNER?

🐾 You train dogs.

🐾 You train people to train dogs.

🐾 You interview people to hire to train dogs.

Listed on the additional pages below you will find countless success stories of real-life clients that we have really helped.

## Additionally if you simply visit:

www.ThrivetimeShow.com/testimonials/ you will also find countless client success stories there as well.

To provide you with a detailed example of what it's like to help business owners to grow their business, I want to first start by stating I love to help good people grow good businesses. Now,

I want to tell you a true story about a client whose business we helped improve and transform dramatically from a stagnant $420,000 year business to a thriving 15+ location business. Before we met this client their business had peaked, it had plateaued and was not growing despite the tireless amount of effort that they had put into trying to grow their business year after year.

This particular client who I am describing found me and the business mentorship that I provide while listening to a business podcast, where I was teaching about the importance of knowing your numbers and building business systems that are repeatable and scalable.

**PAWS**, for a
Notable Quotable

"Without a plan for your life, it is easier to follow the course of least resistance, to go with the flow, to drift with the current with no particular destination in mind. Having a definite plan for your life greatly simplifies the process of making hundreds of daily decisions that affect your ultimate success. When you know where you want to go, you can quickly decide if your actions are moving you toward your goal or away from it. Without definite, precise goals and a plan for their achievement, each decision must be considered in a vacuum. Definiteness of purpose provides context and allows you to relate specific actions to your overall plan."

### - NAPOLEON HILL

*(The best-selling author of Think & Grow Rich, the book that changed my life. Napoleon Hill's writings had such a huge impact on me that I actually named my son Aubrey Napoleon-Hill Clark after Napoleon Hill in honor of the positive and life-changing impact that his writings had on my life.)*

So this client first attended a business workshop where they actually said the following during his conference video testimonial:

> "I definitely learned a lot about life design and making sure the business serves you. The linear workflow for us and getting everything out on paper and documented is really important, our workflows are kind of all over the place. Having a linear workflow and seeing that mapped on multiple different boards is pretty awesome, that's really helpful for me. The atmosphere is awesome, I definitely just stared at the walls figuring out how to make my facility look like this place (Clay designed). This place rocks. It's invigorating, the walls are super, it's just very cool. The atmosphere is cool. The people are nice. I literally want to model it and steal everything that is here at this facility and basically create it just on our business side. Clay is hilarious, I literally laughed so hard that I started having tears yesterday!"

Soon the conference attendee with the stagnant business requested to schedule a one-on-one consultation with me to see if they would be a good fit for the program.

After discovering that they need to make the following updates and more (listed below), I decided to take them on as a client.

- 🐾 **They needed to design a linear workflow.**

- 🐾 **They needed to update the branding of their website.**

- 🐾 **They needed to update the branding of their business cards.**

- 🐾 **They needed to update the branding of their one sheets.**

- They needed to update the branding of everything.

- They needed to have their website optimized.

- They need to learn how to enhance their online reputation.

- They need to develop a no-brainer offer.

- They needed to create effective online advertisements.

- They needed to create a tracking sheet that made sense.

- They needed to have a marketing video scripted, recorded, edited and optimized.

- They needed to create call scripts.

- They needed to learn how to manage phone and customer service sales representatives.

- They needed to install call recording for quality assurance.

- They needed to learn how to host the weekly group interview.

- They needed a place to host their weekly group interview.

- They needed a physical office space to meet their potential new customers (which I gladly provided for them at no additional charge).

- They needed to learn how to create the planning, procedures, policies and checklists needed to scale a business.

- 🐾 **They needed to learn how to manage their accounting systems.**

- 🐾 **They needed to learn how to price their products and services.**

- 🐾 **They needed to learn how to manage their time.**

- 🐾 **They needed to learn how to block out their time effectively.**

- 🐾 **They needed to learn how to fire employees who refuse to follow their systems.**

- 🐾 **They needed to learn how to manage a team (because at the time, the business consisted of the owners and a handful of employees).**

- 🐾 **They needed to learn how to on-board new employees.**

- 🐾 **They needed help finding a quality lawyer.**

- 🐾 **They needed to learn how to optimize their Google map.**

- 🐾 **They needed to learn how to effectively advertise online.**

- 🐾 **They needed help finding key employees.**

- 🐾 **They needed to learn how to host weekly staffing meetings.**

- 🐾 **They needed to learn how to host conferences to educate current, new and potential locations.**

- 🐾 **They needed to learn how to license their business model.**

- 🐾 They needed to find people who were willing to be their initial licensees to test their business model.

- 🐾 They needed to learn what franchising meant.

- 🐾 They needed to learn how to create a franchise disclosure document.

- 🐾 The needed a place to host their annual conference

- 🐾 The needed to learn how to get leads through trade shows

- 🐾 They needed to learn how to create new relationships through the dream 100 sales system

- 🐾 The needed to learn how to simplify pricing packages

- 🐾 They needed to learn how to create a roadmap for their in-person sales meetings

- 🐾 They needed to learn all of this and alot more...

Each week the client would show up for their weekly meeting and I would lead them down the proven path, focusing on improving their business and scaling their systems to the point that 5 months later, this incredible client with the once previously stagnant business, actually said on camera while giving their video testimonial: "What's so great about working with Clay and his team is because they do it all for us! We've been working with Clay for the past 5 months, 2 of which have been our biggest months ever!!!"

Each week, for years I helped this client to grow their business to the point that just 2 years later... This incredibly kind and appreciative client said the following during their video testimonial:

"We just give a huge thank you to Clay and Vanessa Clark. Thank you to Make Your Life Epic! We love you guys and we just appreciate how far you've taken us. This is our old house (pointing at their old house). This is our old neighborhood (pointing at their old neighborhood). So this is my old van and our old school marketing (pointing at the old van). This is our old team, and by team I mean, it's me and another guy. This is our new house, with our new neighborhood. This is our new van with our new marketing. This is our new team. We went from 4 to 14 team members. We went to several different business coaches in the past, and it was all about helping to sell better, but we needed somebody to help us get everything that was in his head out into systems, into manuals and into scripts and actually build a team. So that we have systems in place we have gone from 1 location to 10 locations in only a year. In October of 2016 we grossed $13,000 for the whole month, right now, it's 2018, the month of October, it's only the 22nd, we've already grossed $50,000 for the whole month and we still have time to go. We are just thankful for you and your mentorship and we are really thankful that you guys have helped us to grow a business that we run now instead of the business running us, just thank you, thank you, thank you times 1,000!!!"

Over the years as I've helped thousands of people to build successful businesses, I've found money is just a magnifier, in that it just expands and shows who people really are. When someone is a great person, when you help them to increase their revenue by 10-20 times, it just reveals who they really are. In fact, since 2005, I've discovered people that were just pretending to be nice become exposed for being the nefarious people that they truly are, when they are given copious amounts of money. Truly kind and wonderful people are able to make an even bigger positive impact on the people and world around them when you help them to increase their revenue by 10-20 times.

So, if you are a sincere person who is passionate about growing a successful business by using a proven turn-key business model, I would absolutely love to help you. However, if you are a passive-aggressive and nefarious person, who secretly plots and schemes for your financial benefit, I would love not to speak with you. It is possible to quickly learn how to create both time and financial freedom by building a profitable Make Your Dog Epic dog training business. I love helping good people to create good businesses. To learn more, simply request additional information and schedule a free consultation with me today at www.MakeYourDogEpic.com.

**Clay Clark**
- Founder of MakeYourDogEpic.com

NOTE: Clay Clark is a father of five kids, the former "Young U.S. SBA Entrepreneur of the Year" for the State of Oklahoma, the founder of several multi-million dollar companies, and the host of the ThrivetimeShow podcast which has been number one overall on the iTunes business podcast charts 6 times. Clay Clark is a member of the Forbes Business Coach Council, an Amazon best-selling author and the host of the ThrivetimeShow podcast which has hit #1 on the iTunes charts in the category of business 6 times. Throughout his career he's co-founded / founded several successful organizations including:

www.DJConnection.com | www.EpicPhotos.com | www.EITRLounge.com | Fears & Clark Real Estate Group | www.MakeYourLifeEpic.com | Party Perfect (Which was purchased by Party Pro Rentals) | TipTop K9 Franchising (Clay did not start TipTopK9, but he did co-found TipTopK9 franchising) | www.Thrive15.com (The interactive online entrepreneurship school) | The Tulsa Bridal Association Wedding Show

**Want to open your own Make Your Dog Epic dog training business?** Learn how to have your own! Open one of the most affordable and turn-key dog training businesses on the planet at MakeYourDogEpic.com.

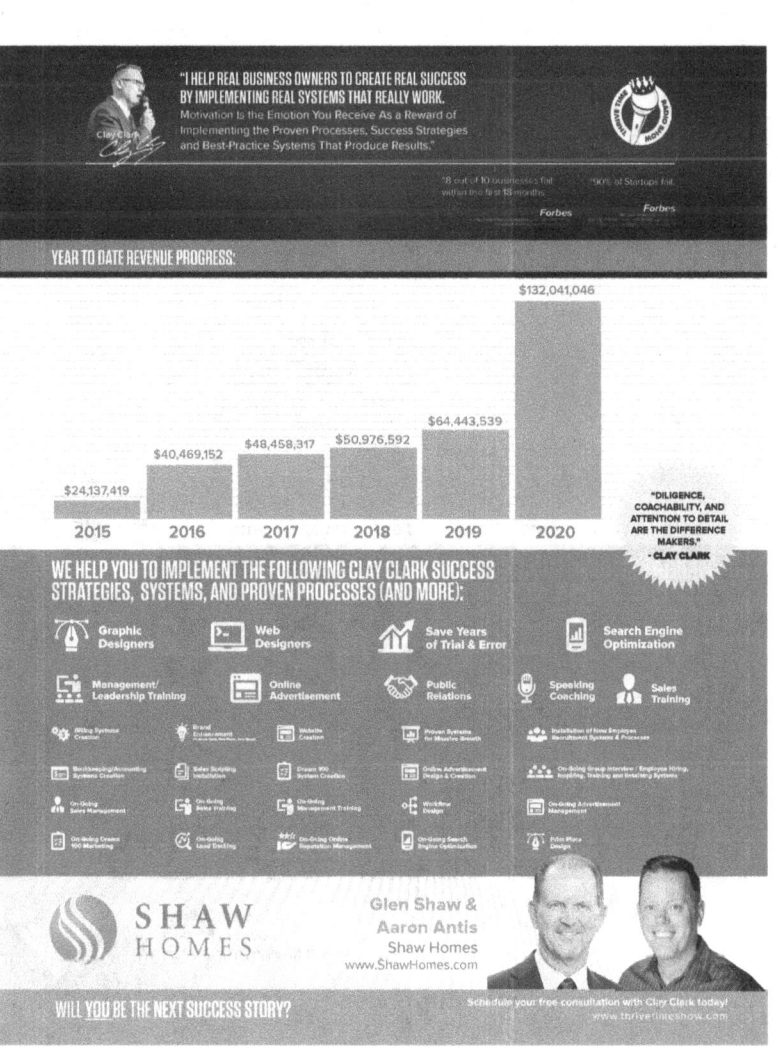

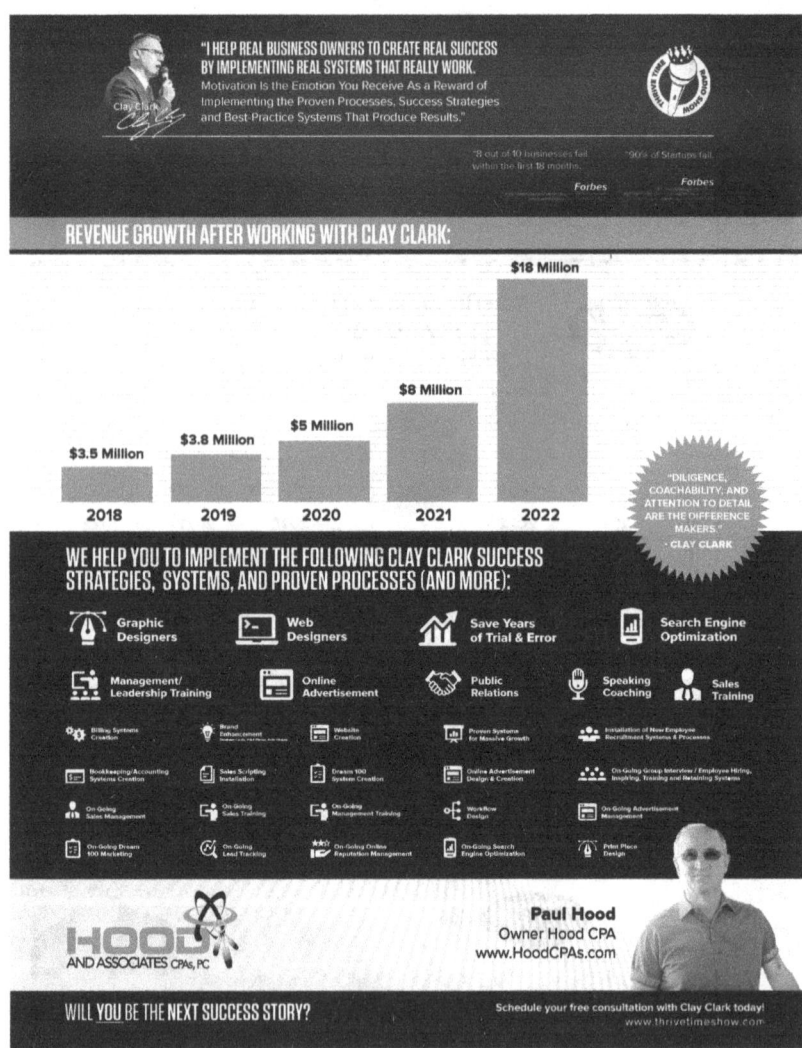

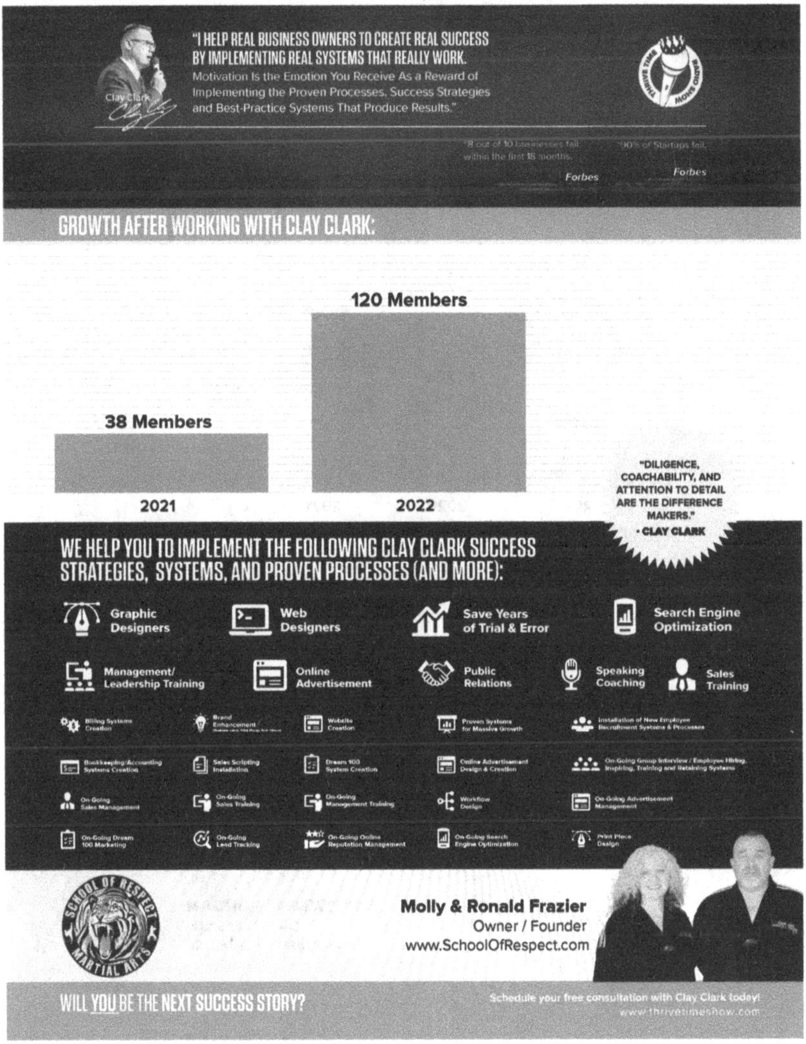

**"I HELP REAL BUSINESS OWNERS TO CREATE REAL SUCCESS BY IMPLEMENTING REAL SYSTEMS THAT REALLY WORK.** Motivation Is the Emotion You Receive As a Reward of Implementing the Proven Processes, Success Strategies and Best-Practice Systems That Produce Results."

Clay Clark

"8 out of 10 businesses fail within the first 18 months. *Forbes*

90% of Startups fail. *Forbes*

## GROWTH AFTER WORKING WITH CLAY CLARK:

**120 Members** — 2022

**38 Members** — 2021

"DILIGENCE, COACHABILITY, AND ATTENTION TO DETAIL ARE THE DIFFERENCE MAKERS." - CLAY CLARK

## WE HELP YOU TO IMPLEMENT THE FOLLOWING CLAY CLARK SUCCESS STRATEGIES, SYSTEMS, AND PROVEN PROCESSES (AND MORE):

- Graphic Designers
- Web Designers
- Save Years of Trial & Error
- Search Engine Optimization
- Management/ Leadership Training
- Online Advertisement
- Public Relations
- Speaking Coaching
- Sales Training
- Billing Systems Creation
- Brand Enhancement
- Website Creation
- Proven Systems for Massive Growth
- Installation of New Employee Recruitment Systems & Processes
- Bookkeeping/Accounting Systems Creation
- Sales Scripting Installation
- Dream 100 System Creation
- Online Advertisement Design & Creation
- On-Going Group Interview / Employee Hiring, Inspiring, Training and Retaining Systems
- On-Going Sales Management
- On-Going Sales Training
- On-Going Management Training
- Workflow Design
- On-Going Advertisement Management
- On-Going Dream 100 Marketing
- On-Going Lead Tracking
- On-Going Online Reputation Management
- On-Going Search Engine Optimization
- Print Piece Design

**Molly & Ronald Frazier**
Owner / Founder
www.SchoolOfRespect.com

**WILL YOU BE THE NEXT SUCCESS STORY?**

Schedule your free consultation with Clay Clark today! www.thrivetimeshow.com

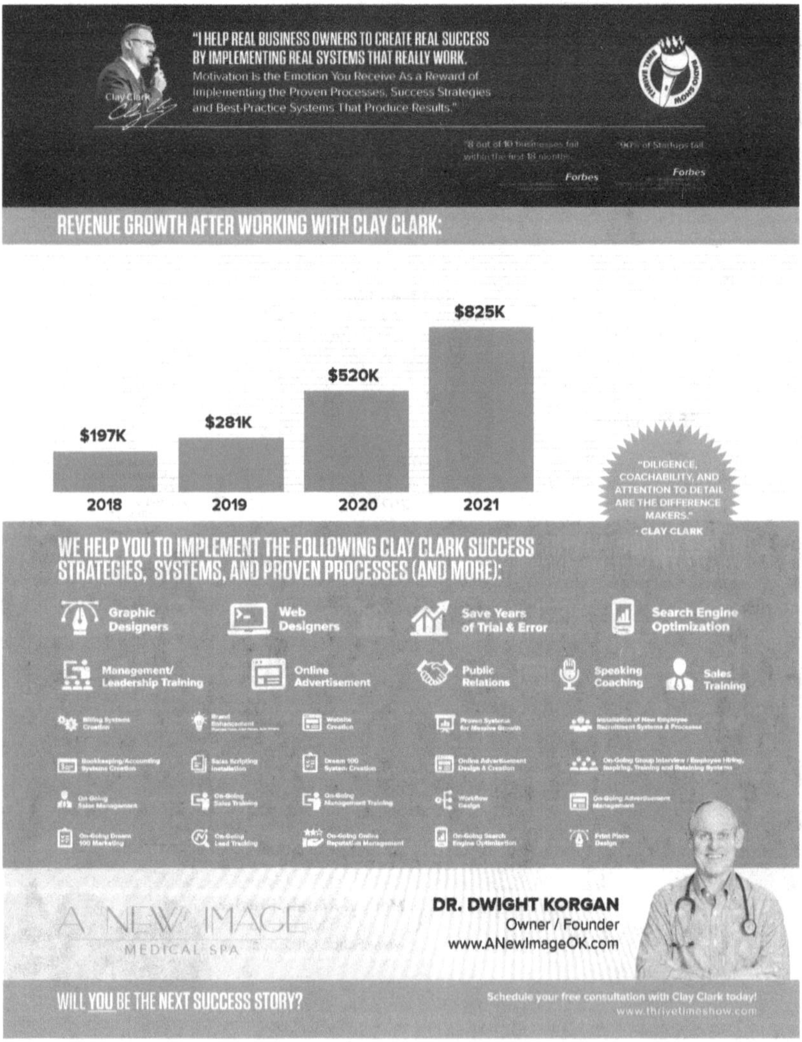

## REVENUE GROWTH AFTER WORKING WITH CLAY CLARK:

- **$197K** — 2018
- **$281K** — 2019
- **$520K** — 2020
- **$825K** — 2021

"DILIGENCE, COACHABILITY, AND ATTENTION TO DETAIL ARE THE DIFFERENCE MAKERS."
- CLAY CLARK

## WE HELP YOU TO IMPLEMENT THE FOLLOWING CLAY CLARK SUCCESS STRATEGIES, SYSTEMS, AND PROVEN PROCESSES (AND MORE):

- Graphic Designers
- Web Designers
- Save Years of Trial & Error
- Search Engine Optimization
- Management/ Leadership Training
- Online Advertisement
- Public Relations
- Speaking Coaching
- Sales Training

**A NEW IMAGE** MEDICAL SPA

**DR. DWIGHT KORGAN**
Owner / Founder
www.ANewImageOK.com

WILL **YOU** BE THE **NEXT SUCCESS STORY?**

Schedule your free consultation with Clay Clark today!
www.thrivetimeshow.com

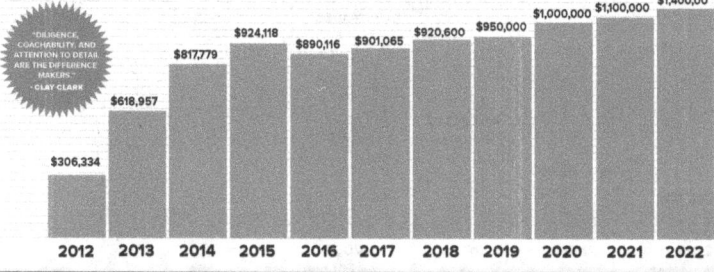

## REVENUE GROWTH AFTER WORKING WITH CLAY CLARK:

| Year | Revenue |
|------|---------|
| 2012 | $306,334 |
| 2013 | $618,957 |
| 2014 | $817,779 |
| 2015 | $924,118 |
| 2016 | $890,116 |
| 2017 | $901,065 |
| 2018 | $920,600 |
| 2019 | $950,000 |
| 2020 | $1,000,000 |
| 2021 | $1,100,000 |
| 2022 | $1,400,00 |

"DILIGENCE, COACHABILITY, AND ATTENTION TO DETAIL ARE THE DIFFERENCE MAKERS." - CLAY CLARK

## WE HELP YOU TO IMPLEMENT THE FOLLOWING CLAY CLARK SUCCESS STRATEGIES, SYSTEMS, AND PROVEN PROCESSES (AND MORE):

- Graphic Designers
- Web Designers
- Save Years of Trial & Error
- Search Engine Optimization
- Management/ Leadership Training
- Online Advertisement
- Public Relations
- Speaking Coaching
- Sales Training

**Kelly Hernelsen**
Owner / Founder
www.westredonsite.com

**WILL YOU BE THE NEXT SUCCESS STORY?**

Schedule your free consultation with Clay Clark today!
www.thrivetimeshow.com

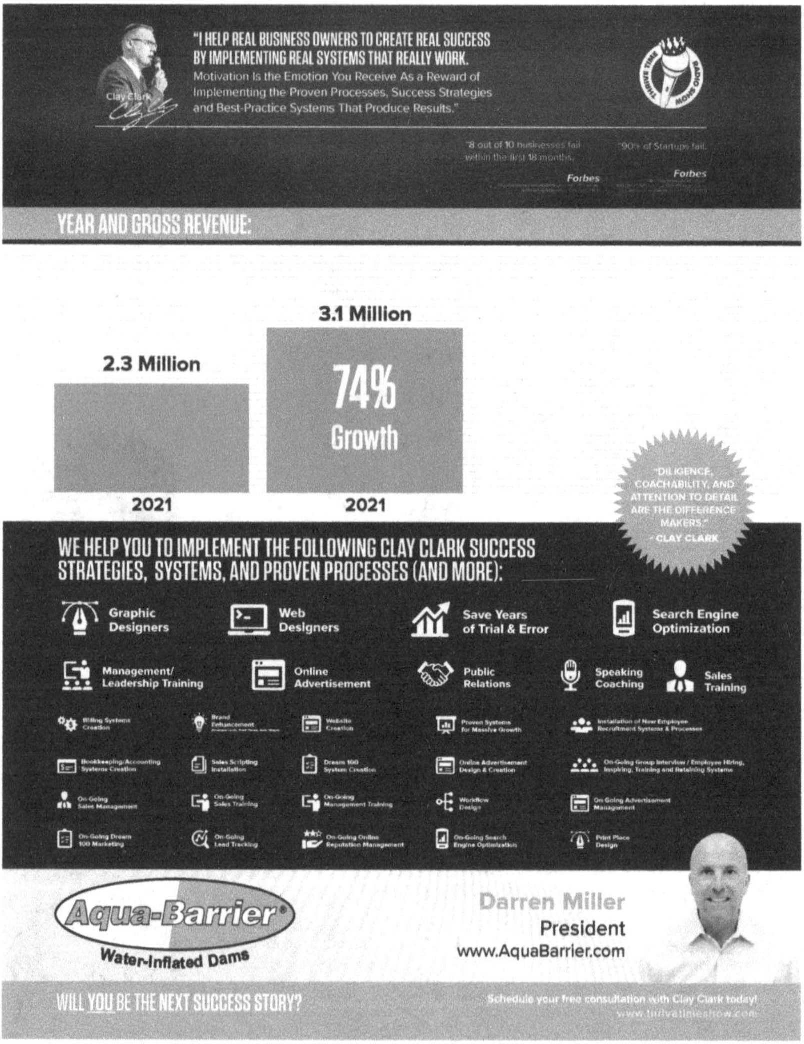

**YEAR AND GROSS REVENUE:**

**2.3 Million** — 2021

**3.1 Million** — 2021
**74% Growth**

"DILIGENCE, COACHABILITY, AND ATTENTION TO DETAIL ARE THE DIFFERENCE MAKERS." - CLAY CLARK

**WE HELP YOU TO IMPLEMENT THE FOLLOWING CLAY CLARK SUCCESS STRATEGIES, SYSTEMS, AND PROVEN PROCESSES (AND MORE):**

- Graphic Designers
- Web Designers
- Save Years of Trial & Error
- Search Engine Optimization
- Management/Leadership Training
- Online Advertisement
- Public Relations
- Speaking Coaching
- Sales Training

**Aqua-Barrier®** Water-Inflated Dams

**Darren Miller**
President
www.AquaBarrier.com

**WILL YOU BE THE NEXT SUCCESS STORY?**

Schedule your free consultation with Clay Clark today!

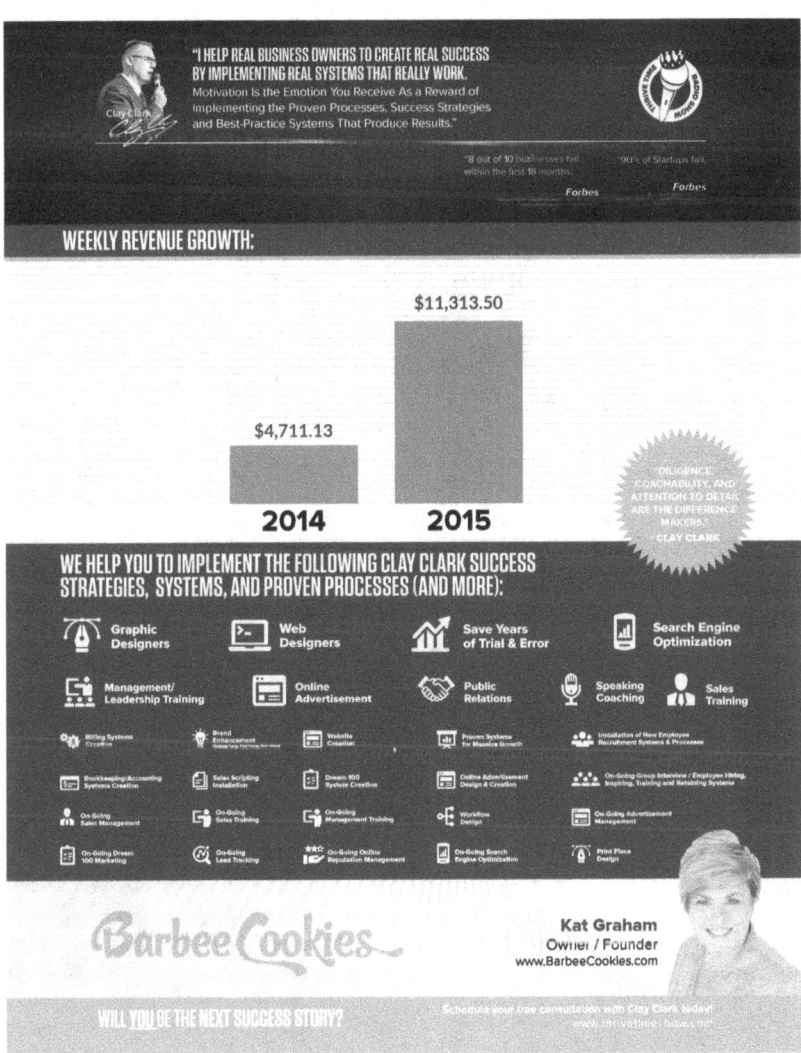

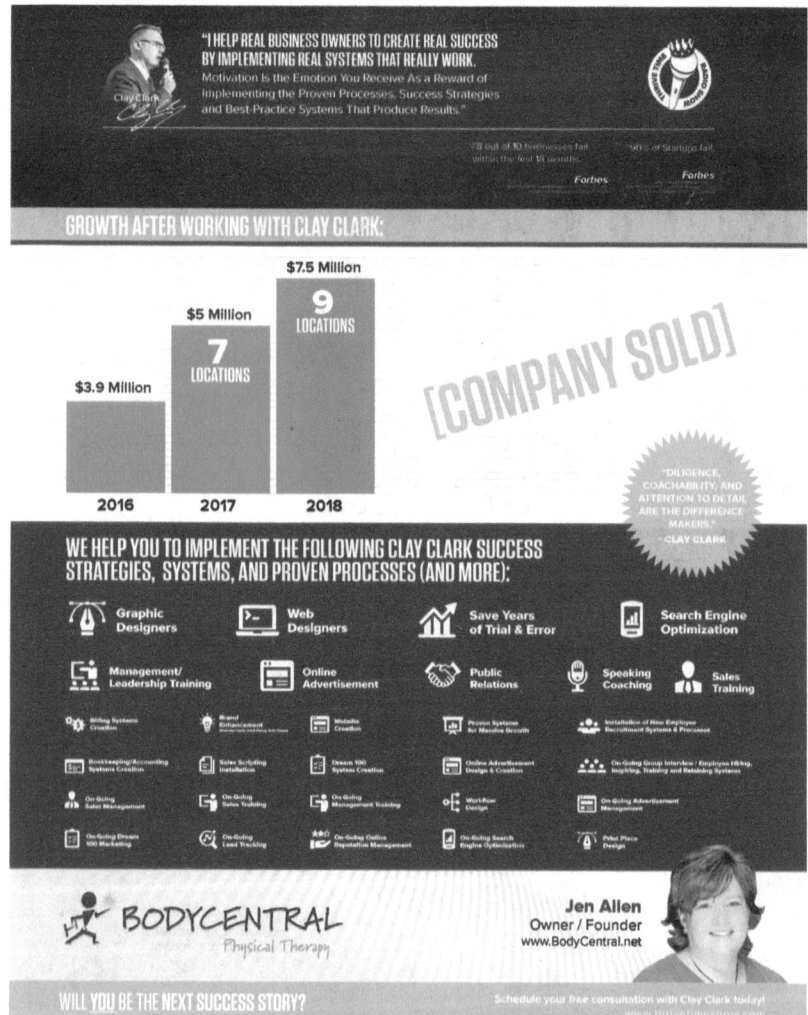

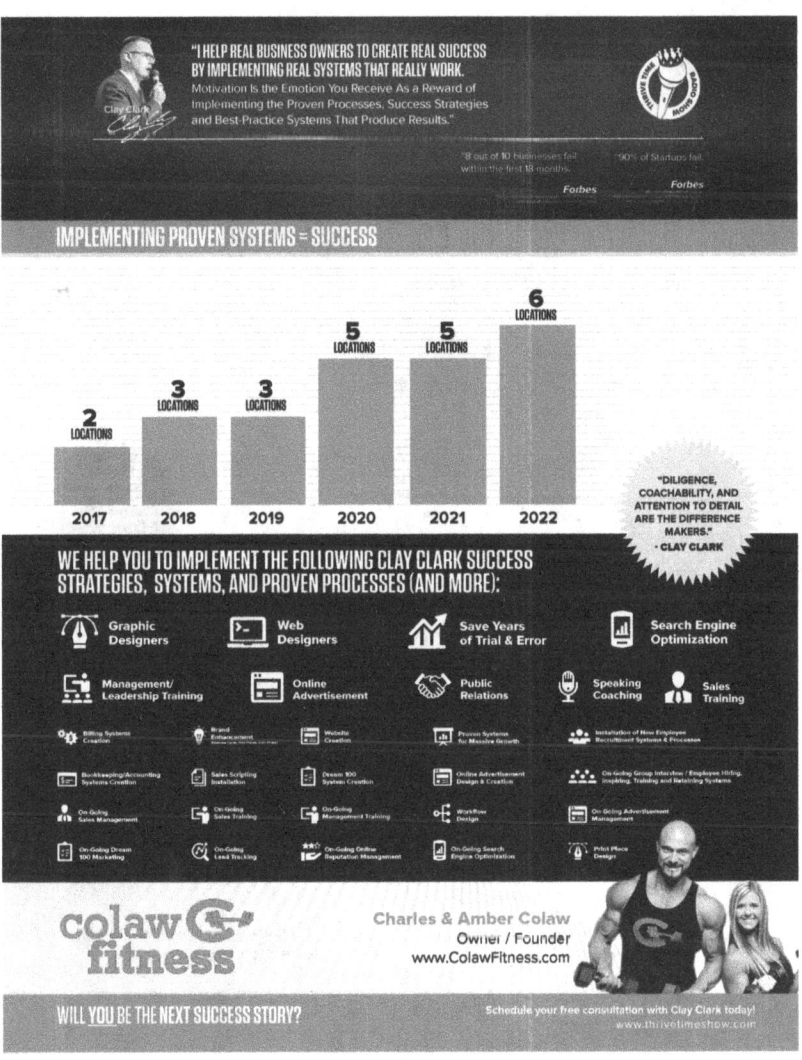

## IMPLEMENTING PROVEN SYSTEMS = SUCCESS

"I HELP REAL BUSINESS OWNERS TO CREATE REAL SUCCESS BY IMPLEMENTING REAL SYSTEMS THAT REALLY WORK."
Motivation Is the Emotion You Receive As a Reward of Implementing the Proven Processes, Success Strategies and Best-Practice Systems That Produce Results."

Clay Clark

"8 out of 10 businesses fail within the first 18 months."
Forbes

"90% of Startups fail."
Forbes

- 2017 — **2** LOCATIONS
- 2018 — **3** LOCATIONS
- 2019 — **3** LOCATIONS
- 2020 — **5** LOCATIONS
- 2021 — **5** LOCATIONS
- 2022 — **6** LOCATIONS

"DILIGENCE, COACHABILITY, AND ATTENTION TO DETAIL ARE THE DIFFERENCE MAKERS."
- CLAY CLARK

## WE HELP YOU TO IMPLEMENT THE FOLLOWING CLAY CLARK SUCCESS STRATEGIES, SYSTEMS, AND PROVEN PROCESSES (AND MORE):

- Graphic Designers
- Web Designers
- Save Years of Trial & Error
- Search Engine Optimization
- Management/ Leadership Training
- Online Advertisement
- Public Relations
- Speaking Coaching
- Sales Training
- Billing Systems Creation
- Brand Enhancement
- Website Creation
- Proven Systems for Massive Growth
- Installation of New Employee Recruitment Systems & Processes
- Bookkeeping/Accounting Systems Creation
- Sales Scripting Installation
- Dream 100 System Creation
- Online Advertisement Design & Creation
- On-Going Group Interactive / Employee Hiring, Inspiring, Training and Retaining Systems
- On-Going Sales Management
- On-Going Sales Training
- On-Going Management Training
- Workflow Design
- On-Going Advertisement Management
- On-Going Dream 100 Marketing
- On-Going Lead Tracking
- On-Going Online Reputation Management
- On-Going Search Engine Optimization
- Print Place Design

## colaw fitness

**Charles & Amber Colaw**
Owner / Founder
www.ColawFitness.com

WILL **YOU** BE THE **NEXT** SUCCESS STORY?

Schedule your free consultation with Clay Clark today!
www.thrivetimeshow.com

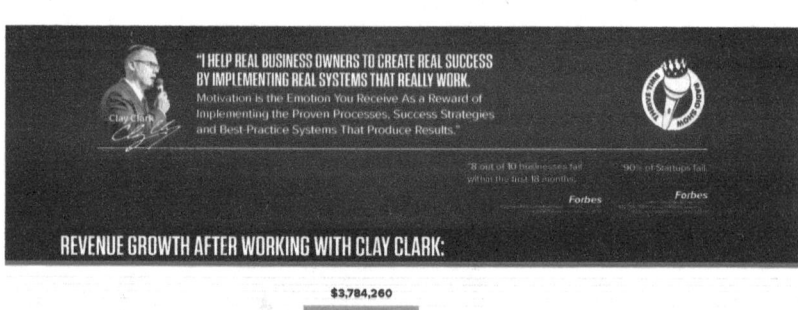

## REVENUE GROWTH AFTER WORKING WITH CLAY CLARK:

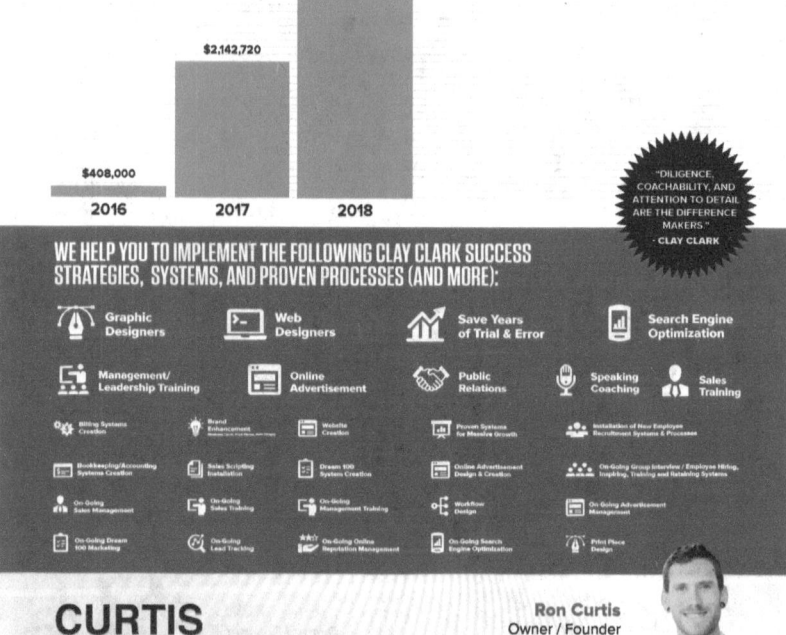

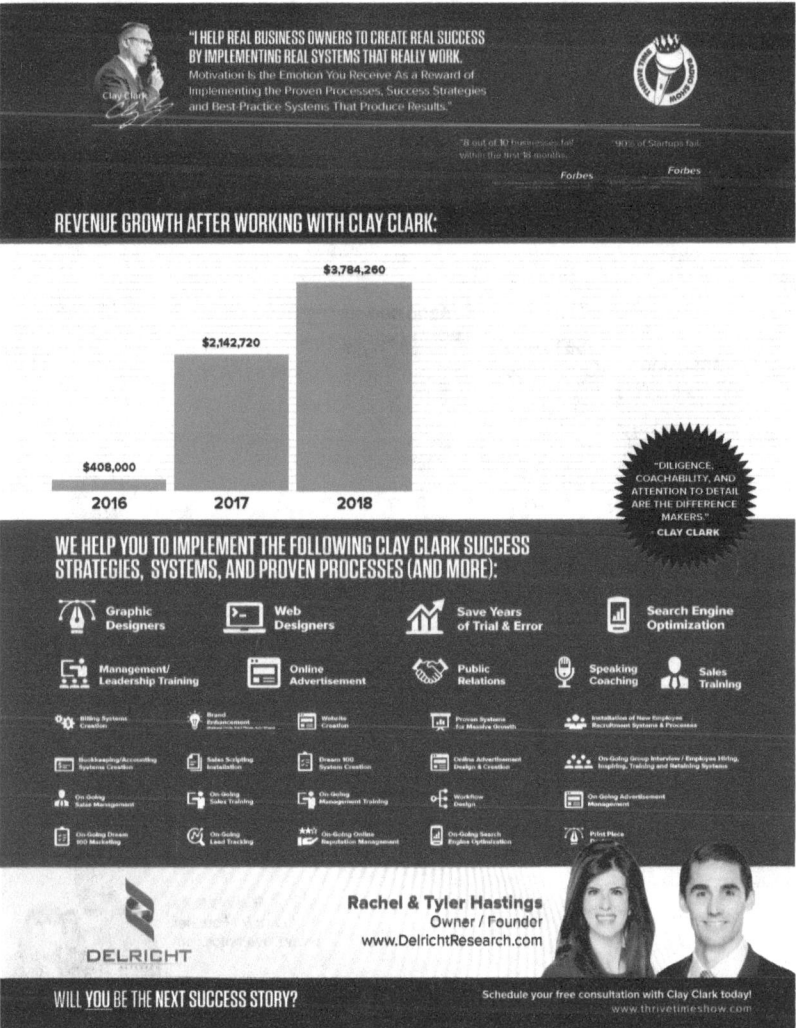

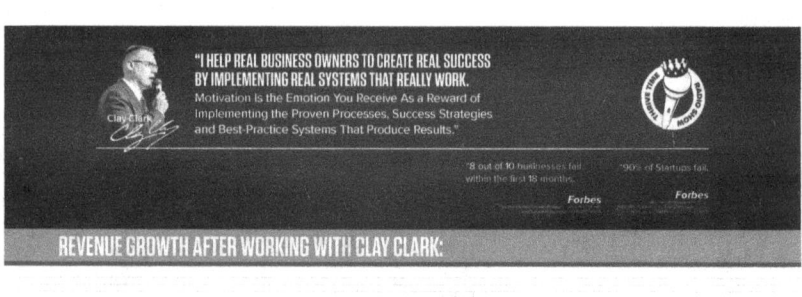

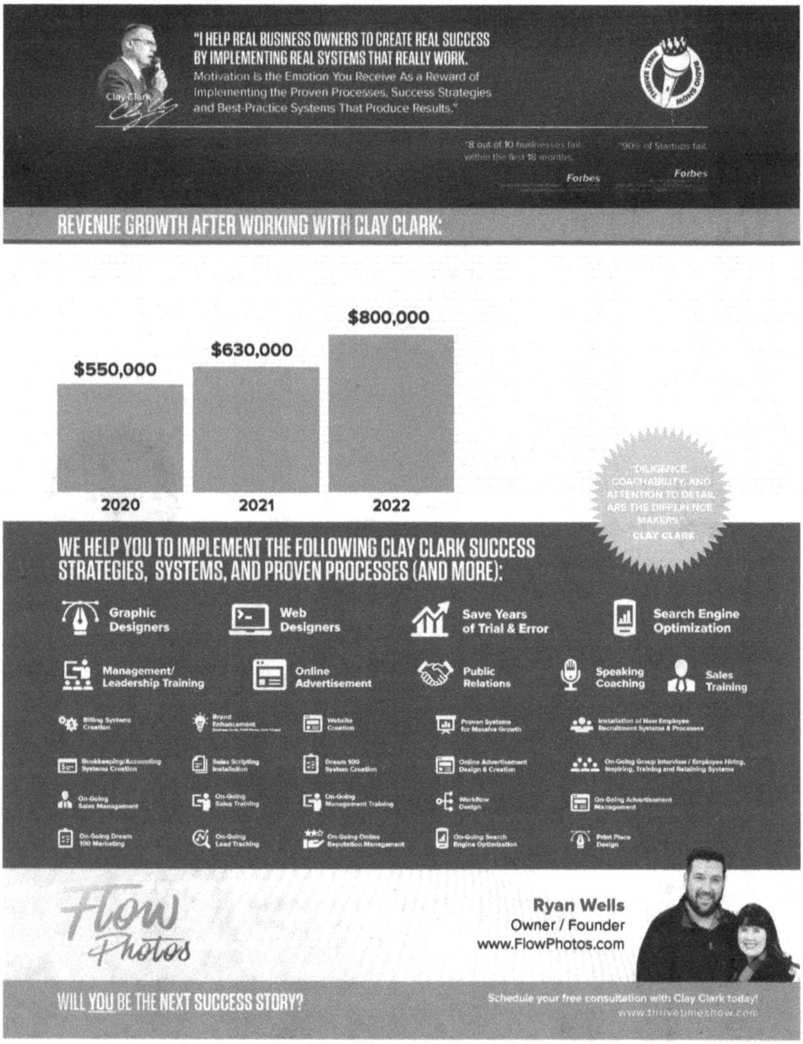

"I HELP REAL BUSINESS OWNERS TO CREATE REAL SUCCESS BY IMPLEMENTING REAL SYSTEMS THAT REALLY WORK.
Motivation Is the Emotion You Receive As a Reward of Implementing the Proven Processes, Success Strategies and Best-Practice Systems That Produce Results."

Clay Clark

"8 out of 10 businesses fail within the first 18 months."
*Forbes*

"90% of Startups fail."
*Forbes*

## REVENUE GROWTH AFTER WORKING WITH CLAY CLARK:

| 2020 | 2021 | 2022 |
|------|------|------|
| $550,000 | $630,000 | $800,000 |

"DILIGENCE, COACHABILITY, AND ATTENTION TO DETAIL, ARE THE DIFFERENCE MAKERS."
- CLAY CLARK

## WE HELP YOU TO IMPLEMENT THE FOLLOWING CLAY CLARK SUCCESS STRATEGIES, SYSTEMS, AND PROVEN PROCESSES (AND MORE):

- Graphic Designers
- Web Designers
- Save Years of Trial & Error
- Search Engine Optimization
- Management/ Leadership Training
- Online Advertisement
- Public Relations
- Speaking Coaching
- Sales Training

- Billing Systems Creation
- Brand Enhancement
- Website Creation
- Proven Systems for Massive Growth
- Installation of New Employee Recruitment Systems & Processes
- Bookkeeping&Accounting Systems Creation
- Sales Scripting Installation
- Dream 100 System Creation
- Online Advertisement Design & Creation
- On-Going Group Interview / Employee Hiring, Inspiring, Training and Retaining Systems
- On-Going Sales Management
- On-Going Sales Training
- On-Going Management Training
- Workflow Design
- On-Going Advertisement Management
- On-Going Dream 100 Marketing
- On-Going Lead Tracking
- On-Going Online Reputation Management
- On-Going Search Engine Optimization
- Print Piece Design

*Flow Photos*

**Ryan Wells**
Owner / Founder
www.FlowPhotos.com

**WILL YOU BE THE NEXT SUCCESS STORY?**

Schedule your free consultation with Clay Clark today!
www.thrivetimeshow.com

165

"I HELP REAL BUSINESS OWNERS TO CREATE REAL SUCCESS BY IMPLEMENTING REAL SYSTEMS THAT REALLY WORK.
Motivation Is the Emotion You Receive As a Reward of Implementing the Proven Processes, Success Strategies and Best-Practice Systems That Produce Results."

Clay Clark

"8 out of 10 businesses fail within the first 18 months."
Forbes

"90% of Startups fail."
Forbes

## IMPLEMENTING PROVEN SYSTEMS = SUCCESS

# 16,000% Growth

"DILIGENCE, COACHABILITY, AND ATTENTION TO DETAIL ARE THE DIFFERENCE MAKERS."
- CLAY CLARK

## WE HELP YOU TO IMPLEMENT THE FOLLOWING CLAY CLARK SUCCESS STRATEGIES, SYSTEMS, AND PROVEN PROCESSES (AND MORE):

 Graphic Designers
 Web Designers
 Save Years of Trial & Error
 Search Engine Optimization

 Management/Leadership Training
 Online Advertisement
 Public Relations
 Speaking Coaching
 Sales Training

 Billing Systems Creation
 Brand Enhancement
 Website Creation
 Proven System for Massive Growth
Installation of New Employee Recruitment Systems & Processes

 Bookkeeping/Accounting Systems Creation
 Sales Scripting Installation
 Dream 100 System Creation
 Online Advertisement Design & Creation
On-Going Group Interview / Employee Hiring, Inspiring, Training and Retaining Systems

 On-Going Sales Management
 On-Going Sales Training
 On-Going Management Training
 Workflow Design
 On-Going Advertisement Management

 On-Going Dream 100 Marketing
 On-Going Lead Tracking
On-Going Online Reputation Management
On-Going Search Engine Optimization
 Print Piece Design

 FLYOVER CONSERVATIVES

**David & Stacy Whited**
Owners / Founders
www.FlyoverConservatives.com

WILL **YOU** BE THE **NEXT SUCCESS STORY?**

Schedule your free consultation with Clay Clark today!
www.thrivetimeshow.com

**"I HELP REAL BUSINESS OWNERS TO CREATE REAL SUCCESS BY IMPLEMENTING REAL SYSTEMS THAT REALLY WORK.**
Motivation Is the Emotion You Receive As a Reward of Implementing the Proven Processes, Success Strategies and Best Practice Systems That Produce Results."

Clay Clark

"8 out of 10 businesses fail within the first 18 months."
*Forbes*

"90% of Startups fail."
*Forbes*

## REVENUE GROWTH AFTER WORKING WITH CLAY CLARK:

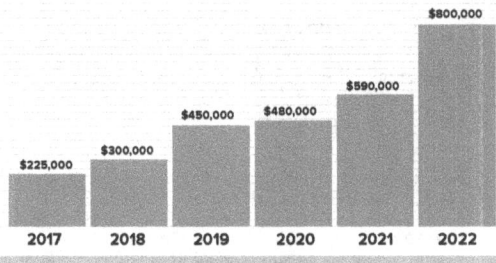

| 2017 | 2018 | 2019 | 2020 | 2021 | 2022 |
|------|------|------|------|------|------|
| $225,000 | $300,000 | $450,000 | $480,000 | $590,000 | $800,000 |

"DILIGENCE, COACHABILITY, AND ATTENTION TO DETAIL ARE THE DIFFERENCE MAKERS."
- CLAY CLARK

## WE HELP YOU TO IMPLEMENT THE FOLLOWING CLAY CLARK SUCCESS STRATEGIES, SYSTEMS, AND PROVEN PROCESSES (AND MORE):

 Graphic Designers

 Web Designers

 Save Years of Trial & Error

 Search Engine Optimization

Management/ Leadership Training

Online Advertisement

Public Relations

Speaking Coaching

Sales Training

**the HUB**
24/7 fitness center

Luke Owens
Owner / Founder
www.TheHubGym.com

**WILL YOU BE THE NEXT SUCCESS STORY?**

Schedule your free consultation with Clay Clark today!
www.thrivetimeshow.com

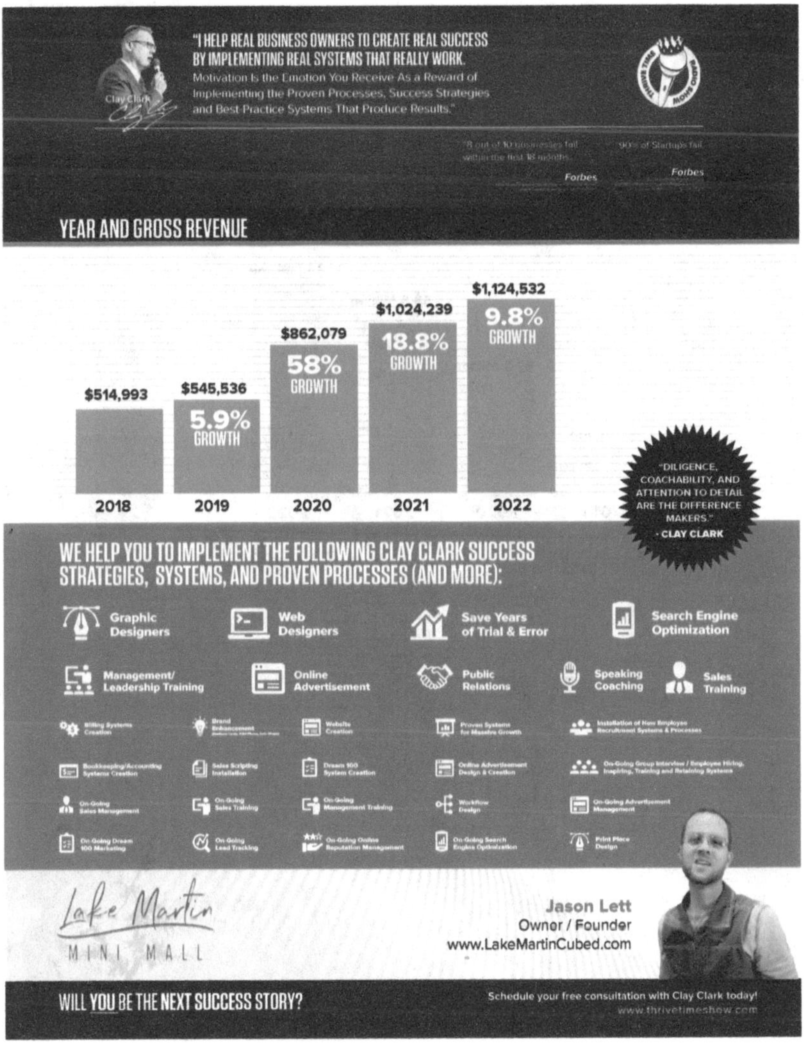


**Want to open your own Make Your Dog Epic dog training business?** Learn how to have your own! Open one of the most affordable and turn-key dog training businesses on the planet at MakeYourDogEpic.com.

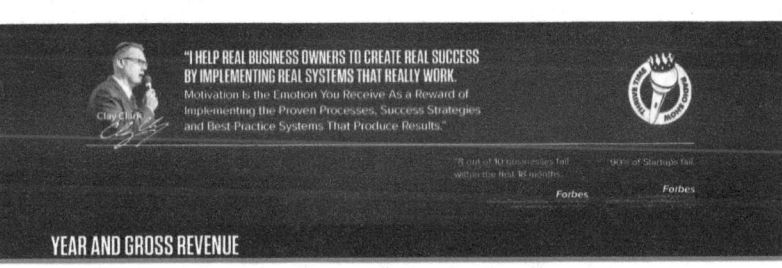

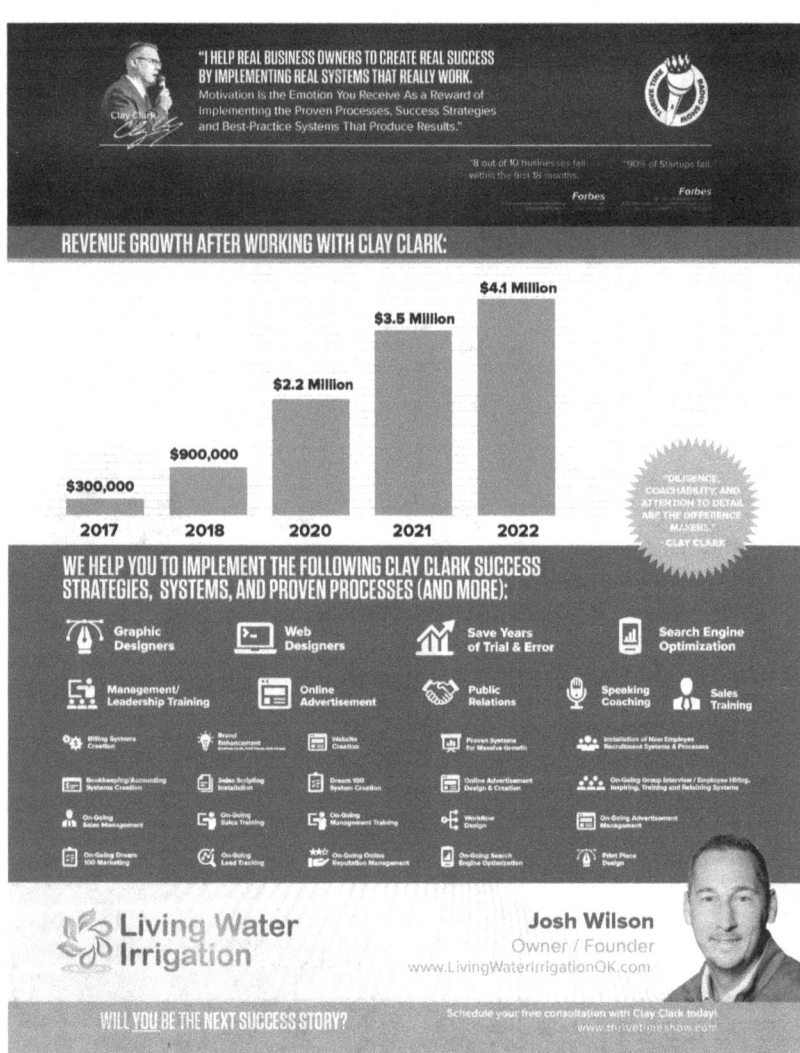

"I HELP REAL BUSINESS OWNERS TO CREATE REAL SUCCESS BY IMPLEMENTING REAL SYSTEMS THAT REALLY WORK.
Motivation Is the Emotion You Receive As a Reward of Implementing the Proven Processes. Success Strategies and Best-Practice Systems That Produce Results."

Clay Clark

"8 out of 10 businesses fail within the first 18 months.

*Forbes*

"90% of Startups fail.

*Forbes*

**YEAR TO DATE REVENUE PROGRESS:**

**79.45%**
Growth Rate

**73**
New Patients

2016    2017

"We have seen a marked increase in the number of new patients we are seeing every month."

- Doctor Mark Morrow

"DILIGENCE, COACHABILITY, AND ATTENTION TO DETAIL ARE THE DIFFERENCE MAKERS."
CLAY CLARK

**SYSTEMS SUCCESSFULLY IMPLEMENTED:**

Graphic Designers

Web Designers

Save Years of Trial & Error

Search Engine Optimization

Management/ Leadership Training

Online Advertisement

Public Relations

Speaking Coaching

Sales Training

 Sitting Systems Creation

 Brand Enhancement

Website Creation

 Proven Systems for Massive Growth

 Introduction of New Employee Recruitment Systems & Processes

Bookkeeping/Accounting Systems Creation

 Sales Scripting Installation

Dream 100 System Creation

 Online Advertisement Design & Creation

 On-Going Group Interview / Employee Hiring, Inspiring, Training and Retaining Systems

On-Going Sales Management

 On-Going Sales Training

 On-Going Management Training

 Workflow Design

On-Going Advertisement Management

On-Going Dream 100 Marketing

 On-Going Lead Tracking

On-Going Online Reputation Management

On-Going Search Engine Optimization

 Print Piece Design

MORROW, LAI, & KITTERMAN
PEDIATRIC DENTISTRY

**Doctor Mark Morrow**
Owner / Founder
www.MLKDentistry.com

 **WILL YOU BE THE NEXT SUCCESS STORY?**

Schedule your free consultation with Clay Clark today!

"I HELP REAL BUSINESS OWNERS TO CREATE REAL SUCCESS BY IMPLEMENTING REAL SYSTEMS THAT REALLY WORK.

Motivation Is the Emotion You Receive As a Reward of Implementing the Proven Processes, Success Strategies and Best-Practice Systems That Produce Results."

Clay Clark

"8 out of 10 businesses fail within the first 18 months."

*Forbes*

"90% of Startups fail."

*Forbes*

## REVENUE GROWTH AFTER WORKING WITH CLAY CLARK

$937,000

$1,500,00

2018

2019

"DILIGENCE, COACHABILITY, AND ATTENTION TO DETAIL ARE THE DIFFERENCE MAKERS."
- CLAY CLARK

## WE HELP YOU TO IMPLEMENT THE FOLLOWING CLAY CLARK SUCCESS STRATEGIES, SYSTEMS, AND PROVEN PROCESSES (AND MORE):

 **Graphic Designers**

 **Web Designers**

 **Save Years of Trial & Error**

 **Search Engine Optimization**

 **Management/ Leadership Training**

 **Online Advertisement**

 **Public Relations**

 **Speaking Coaching**

**Sales Training**

 Billing Systems Creation

Brand Enhancement

Website Creation

Proven Systems for Massive Growth

Installation of New Employee Recruitment Systems & Processes

Bookkeeping/Accounting Systems Creation

 Sales Scripting Installation

 Dream 100 System Creation

Online Advertisement Design & Creation

 On-Going Group Interview / Employee Hiring, Inspiring, Training and Retaining Systems

On-Going Sales Management

On-Going Sales Training

On-Going Management Training

 Workflow Design

On-Going Advertisement Management

 On-Going Dream 100 Marketing

On-Going Lead Tracking

On-Going Online Reputation Management

 On-Going Search Engine Optimization

Print Piece Design

MORNING GLORY

**Dave & Trisha Rich**
Owner / Founder
www.MorningGloryEatery.com

WILL **YOU** BE THE NEXT SUCCESS STORY?

Schedule your free consultation with Clay Clark today!

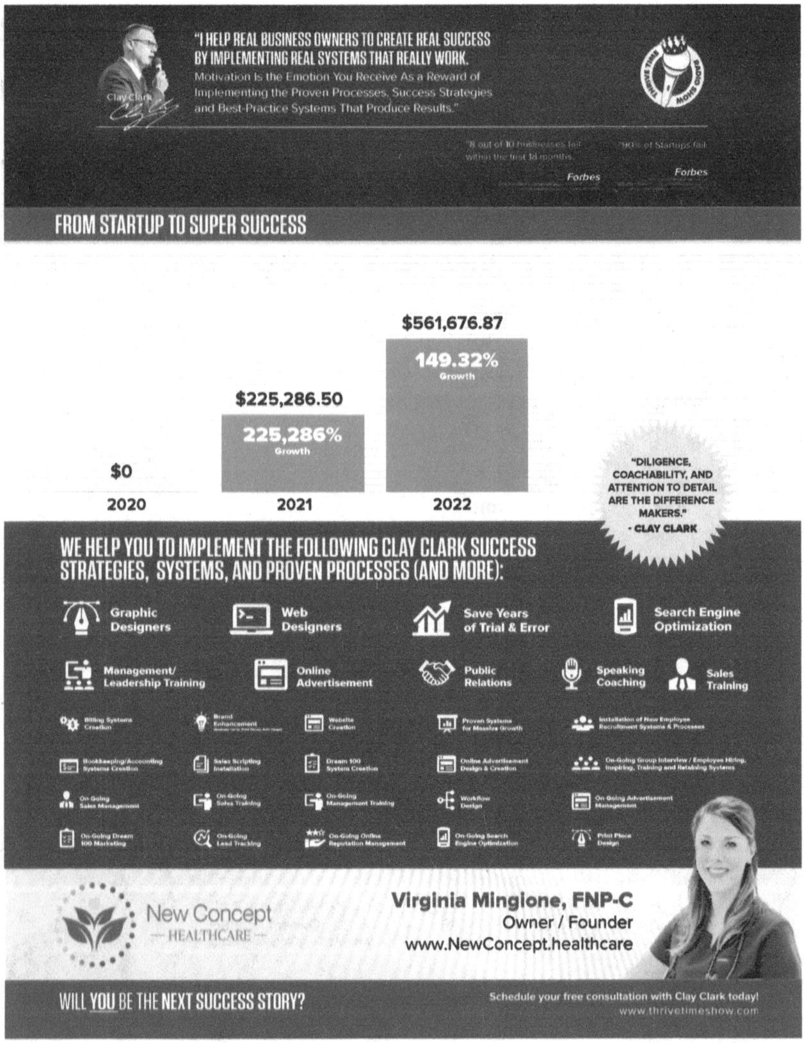

**FROM STARTUP TO SUPER SUCCESS**

$561,676.87

149.32%
Growth

$225,286.50

225,286%
Growth

$0

| 2020 | 2021 | 2022 |

"DILIGENCE, COACHABILITY, AND ATTENTION TO DETAIL ARE THE DIFFERENCE MAKERS."
· CLAY CLARK

## WE HELP YOU TO IMPLEMENT THE FOLLOWING CLAY CLARK SUCCESS STRATEGIES, SYSTEMS, AND PROVEN PROCESSES (AND MORE):

- Graphic Designers
- Web Designers
- Save Years of Trial & Error
- Search Engine Optimization
- Management/ Leadership Training
- Online Advertisement
- Public Relations
- Speaking Coaching
- Sales Training
- Billing Systems Creation
- Brand Enhancement
- Website Creation
- Proven Systems for Massive Growth
- Installation of New Employee Recruitment Systems & Processes
- Bookkeeping/Accounting Systems Creation
- Sales Scripting Installation
- Dream 100 Systems Creation
- Online Advertisement Design & Creation
- On-Going Group Interview / Employee Hiring, Inspiring, Training and Retaining Systems
- On Going Sales Management
- On-Going Sales Training
- On-Going Management Training
- Workflow Design
- On Going Advertisement Management
- On-Going Dream 100 Marketing
- On-Going Lead Tracking
- On-Going Online Reputation Management
- On Going Search Engine Optimization
- Print Piece Design

New Concept
— HEALTHCARE —

**Virginia Mingione, FNP-C**
Owner / Founder
www.NewConcept.healthcare

WILL **YOU** BE THE **NEXT SUCCESS STORY?**

Schedule your free consultation with Clay Clark today!
www.thrivetimeshow.com

## TESTIMONIAL

"Oral Roberts University - "You certainly were the on-site leader that we needed for this calling campaign. By watching you work with these students and seeing the result, I became reassured that hiring you to do exactly what you did was the right thing to do. Your team brought in over $120K in gifts and pledges, which may be an all-time ORU phonathon record! But I'll have more for you later. Again, thanks for everything....and don't drink too much Red Bull!"

**JESSE D. PISORS**
B.A. (1996) M.A. (2005) – Director of Alumni & Ministerial Relations and Annual Fund – Oral Roberts University

"DILIGENCE, COACHABILITY, AND ATTENTION TO DETAIL ARE THE DIFFERENCE MAKERS."
· CLAY CLARK

**SYSTEMS SUCCESSFULLY IMPLEMENTED:**

- Graphic Designers
- Web Designers
- Save Years of Trial & Error
- Search Engine Optimization
- Management/ Leadership Training
- Online Advertisement
- Public Relations
- Speaking Coaching
- Sales Training

**ORU** ORAL ROBERTS UNIVERSITY

**Dr. Jesse Pisors**
Vice President for University Advancement and External Relations
www.ORU.edu

WILL **YOU** BE THE NEXT SUCCESS STORY?

Schedule your free consultation with Clay Clark today!
www.thrivetimeshow.com

"I HELP REAL BUSINESS OWNERS TO CREATE REAL SUCCESS BY IMPLEMENTING REAL SYSTEMS THAT REALLY WORK.
Motivation Is the Emotion You Receive As a Reward of Implementing the Proven Processes, Success Strategies and Best-Practice Systems That Produce Results."

Clay Clark

"8 out of 10 businesses fail within the first 18 months.
*Forbes*

"90% of Startups fail.
*Forbes*

## WEEKLY REVENUE GROWTH:

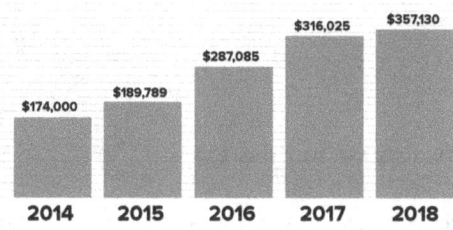

| 2014 | 2015 | 2016 | 2017 | 2018 |
|------|------|------|------|------|
| $174,000 | $189,789 | $287,085 | $316,025 | $357,130 |

"DILIGENCE, COACHABILITY, AND ATTENTION TO DETAIL ARE THE DIFFERENCE MAKERS."
- CLAY CLARK

## WE HELP YOU TO IMPLEMENT THE FOLLOWING CLAY CLARK SUCCESS STRATEGIES, SYSTEMS, AND PROVEN PROCESSES (AND MORE):

 Graphic Designers
 Web Designers
 Save Years of Trial & Error
 Search Engine Optimization

Management/Leadership Training
Online Advertisement
Public Relations
Speaking Coaching
Sales Training

 **PLATINUM** PEST & LAWN

Jared & Jennifer Johnson
Owner / Founder
www.PlatinumPestandLawn.com

WILL **YOU** BE THE NEXT SUCCESS STORY?

Schedule your free consultation with Clay Clark today!
www.thrivetimeshow.com

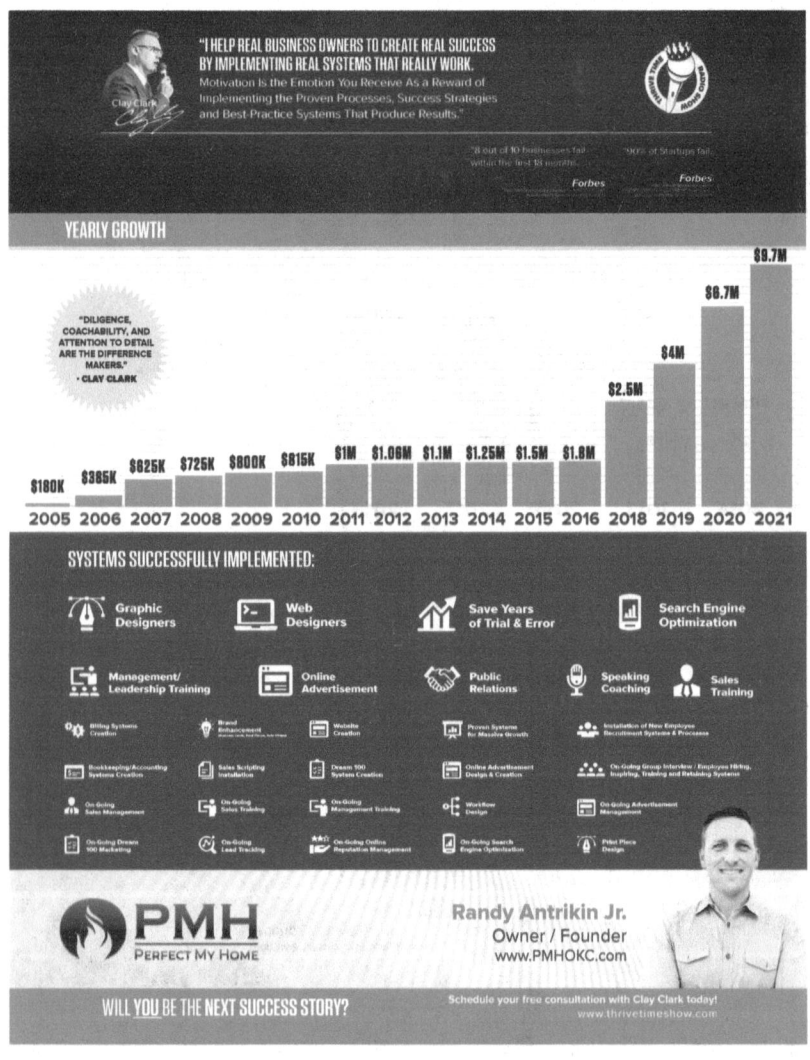

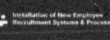

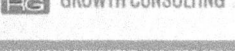

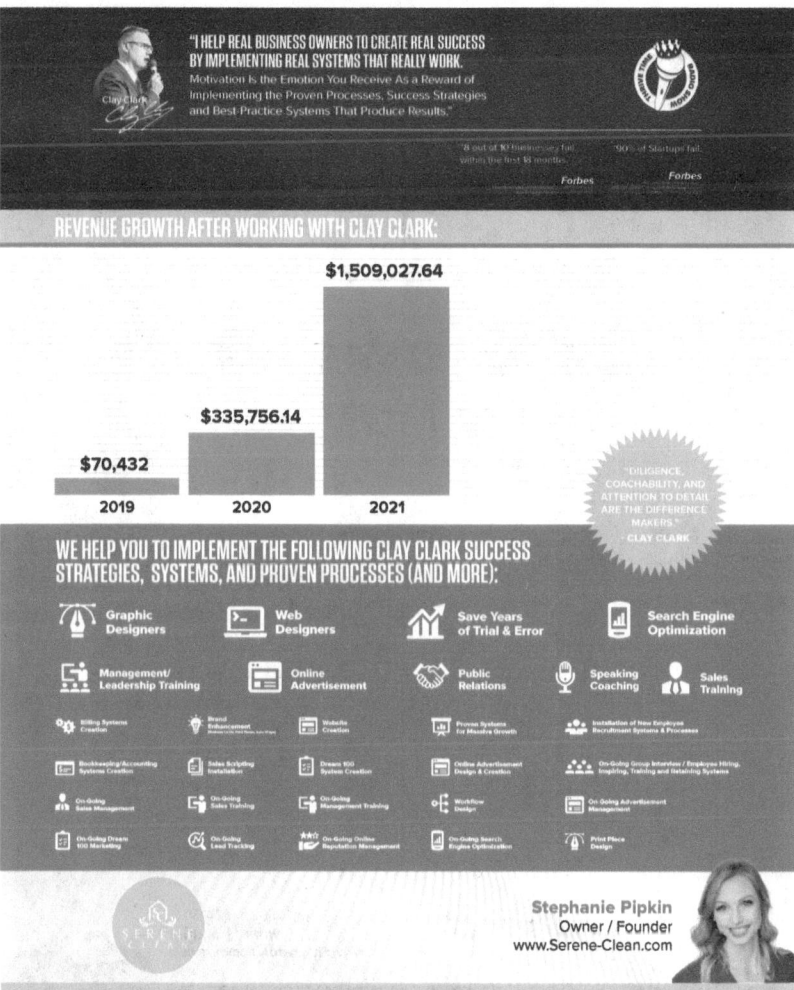

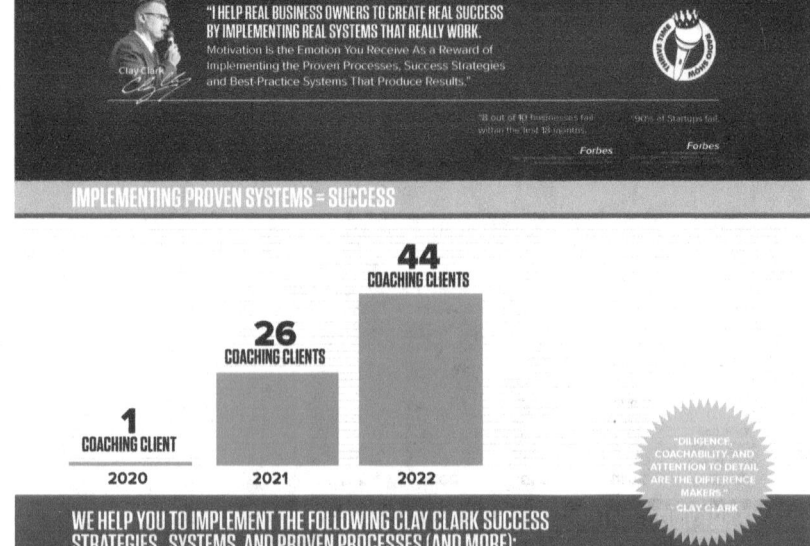

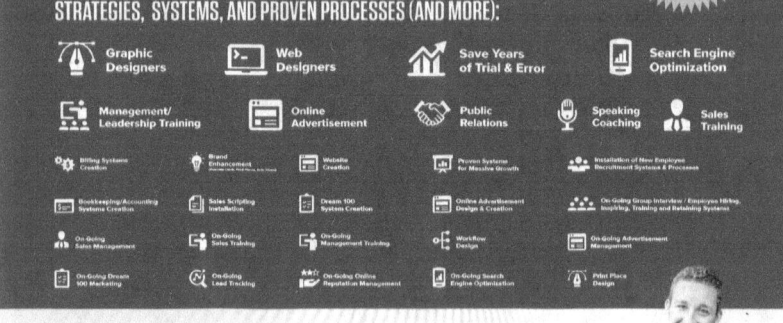

## From start to $24 million of gross sales (in just 18 months)

"From the very start everything that we do is a direct line from Clay and his team and all that they've done for us."

- Danielle Sprik

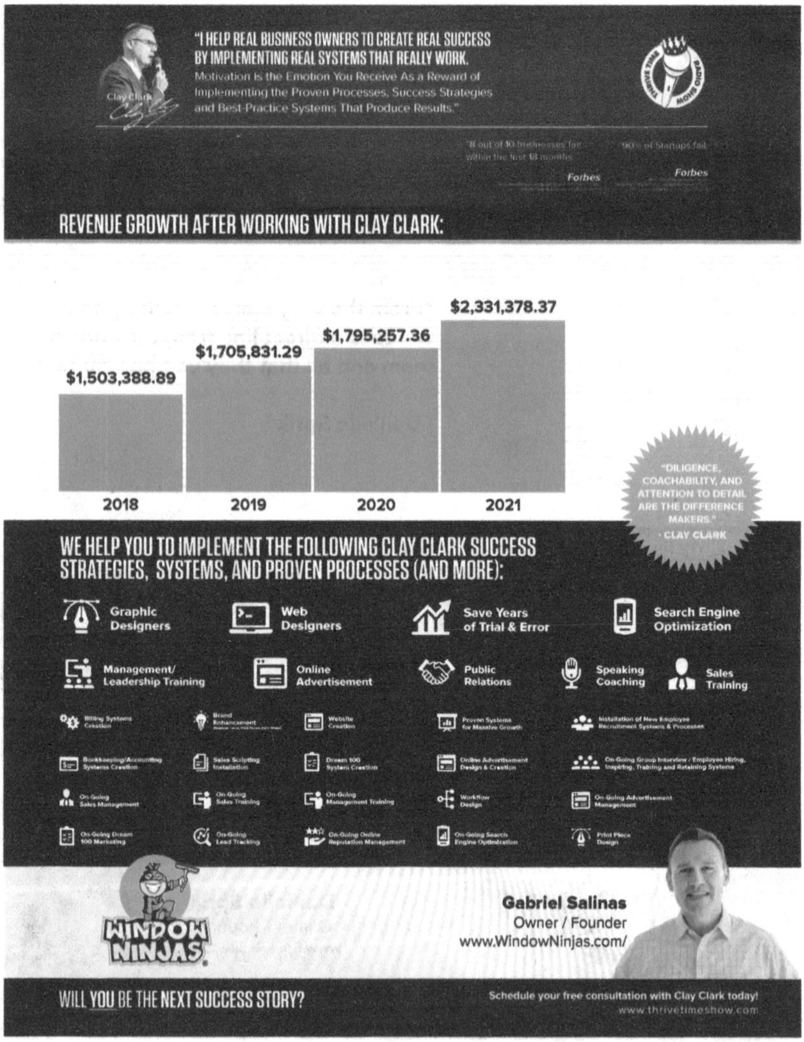

"I HELP REAL BUSINESS OWNERS TO CREATE REAL SUCCESS BY IMPLEMENTING REAL SYSTEMS THAT REALLY WORK. Motivation is the Emotion You Receive As a Reward of Implementing the Proven Processes, Success Strategies and Best-Practice Systems That Produce Results."

Clay Clark

## REVENUE GROWTH AFTER WORKING WITH CLAY CLARK:

- $1,503,388.89 — 2018
- $1,705,831.29 — 2019
- $1,795,257.36 — 2020
- $2,331,378.37 — 2021

"DILIGENCE, COACHABILITY, AND ATTENTION TO DETAIL ARE THE DIFFERENCE MAKERS." - CLAY CLARK

## WE HELP YOU TO IMPLEMENT THE FOLLOWING CLAY CLARK SUCCESS STRATEGIES, SYSTEMS, AND PROVEN PROCESSES (AND MORE):

- Graphic Designers
- Web Designers
- Save Years of Trial & Error
- Search Engine Optimization
- Management/Leadership Training
- Online Advertisement
- Public Relations
- Speaking Coaching
- Sales Training

**Gabriel Salinas**
Owner / Founder
www.WindowNinjas.com/

WINDOW NINJAS

WILL YOU BE THE NEXT SUCCESS STORY?

Schedule your free consultation with Clay Clark today!
www.thrivetimeshow.com

"I HELP REAL BUSINESS OWNERS TO CREATE REAL SUCCESS BY IMPLEMENTING REAL SYSTEMS THAT REALLY WORK." Motivation is the Emotion You Receive As a Reward of Implementing the Proven Processes, Success Strategies and Best-Practice Systems That Produce Results."

Clay Clark

8 out of 10 businesses fail within the first 18 months.
Forbes

90% of Startups fail.
Forbes

**YEARLY GROSS REVENUE GROWTH**

# 75% Growth Rate
## IN 20 MONTHS

"DILIGENCE, COACHABILITY, AND ATTENTION TO DETAIL ARE THE DIFFERENCE MAKERS."
- CLAY CLARK

**WE HELP YOU TO IMPLEMENT THE FOLLOWING CLAY CLARK SUCCESS STRATEGIES, SYSTEMS, AND PROVEN PROCESSES (AND MORE):**

 Graphic Designers

 Web Designers

 Save Years of Trial & Error

 Search Engine Optimization

Management/ Leadership Training

Online Advertisement

Public Relations

Speaking Coaching

Sales Training

Billing Systems Creation

Brand Enhancement

Website Creation

Proven Systems for Massive Growth

Installation of New Employee Recruitment Systems & Processes

Bookkeeping/Accounting Systems Creation

Sales Scripting Installation

Dream 100 System Creation

Online Advertisement Design & Creation

On-Going Group Interview / Employee Hiring, Inspiring, Training and Retaining Systems

On-Going Sales Management

On-Going Sales Training

On-Going Management Training

Workflow Design

On-Going Advertisement Management

On-Going Dream 100 Marketing

On-Going Lead Tracking

On-Going Online Reputation Management

On-Going Search Engine Optimization

Print Piece Design

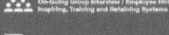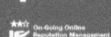

  OILERS TULSA

**Taylor Hall**
General Manager
www.TulsaOilers.com

**WILL YOU BE THE NEXT SUCCESS STORY?**

Schedule your free consultation with Clay Clark today!
www.thrivetimeshow.com

## YEAR-TO-YEAR CONSISTENT GROWTH

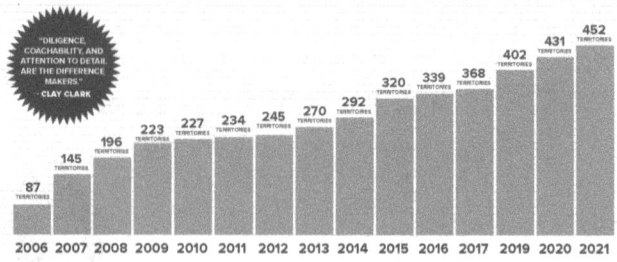

## REVENUE GROWTH AFTER WORKING WITH CLAY CLARK:

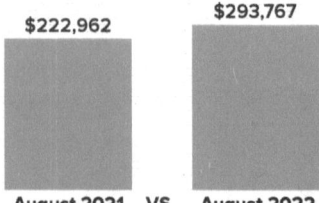

$222,962     $293,767

**August 2021**   VS.   **August 2022**

"DILIGENCE, COACHABILITY, AND ATTENTION TO DETAIL ARE THE DIFFERENCE MAKERS."
- CLAY CLARK

## WE HELP YOU TO IMPLEMENT THE FOLLOWING CLAY CLARK SUCCESS STRATEGIES, SYSTEMS, AND PROVEN PROCESSES (AND MORE):

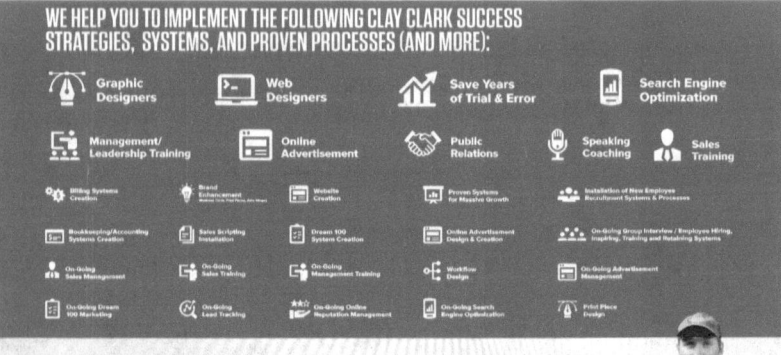

- Graphic Designers
- Web Designers
- Save Years of Trial & Error
- Search Engine Optimization
- Management/Leadership Training
- Online Advertisement
- Public Relations
- Speaking Coaching
- Sales Training

**Tim Scott**
Owners / Founders
www.LegacyLandscapeOK.com

WILL **YOU** BE THE **NEXT SUCCESS STORY?**

Schedule your free consultation with Clay Clark today!
www.thrivetimeshow.com

"I HELP REAL BUSINESS OWNERS TO CREATE REAL SUCCESS BY IMPLEMENTING REAL SYSTEMS THAT REALLY WORK. Motivation Is the Emotion You Receive As a Reward of Implementing the Proven Processes, Success Strategies and Best-Practice Systems That Produce Results."

Clay Clark

"8 out of 10 businesses fail within the first 18 months."
Forbes

"90% of Startups fail.
Forbes

## REVENUE GROWTH AFTER WORKING WITH CLAY CLARK :

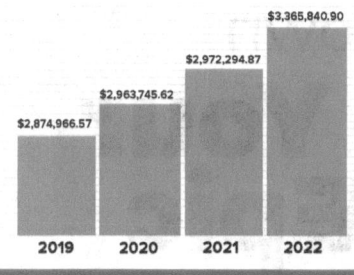

- $3,365,840.90 (2022)
- $2,972,294.87 (2021)
- $2,963,745.62 (2020)
- $2,874,966.57 (2019)

"DILIGENCE, COACHABILITY, AND ATTENTION TO DETAIL ARE THE DIFFERENCE MAKERS."
- CLAY CLARK

## WE HELP YOU TO IMPLEMENT THE FOLLOWING CLAY CLARK SUCCESS STRATEGIES, SYSTEMS, AND PROVEN PROCESSES (AND MORE):

 Graphic Designers

 Web Designers

 Save Years of Trial & Error

 Search Engine Optimization

 Management/ Leadership Training

 Online Advertisement

 Public Relations

 Speaking Coaching — Sales Training

 Billing Systems Creation

 Brand Enhancement

 Website Creation

 Proven Systems for Massive Growth

 Installation of New Employee Recruitment Systems & Processes

 Bookkeeping/Accounting Systems Creation — Sales Scripting Installation — Dream 100 System Creation — Online Advertisement Design & Creation — On-Going Group Interview / Employee Hiring, Inspiring, Training and Retaining Systems

 On-Going Sales Management

 On-Going Sales Training

 On-Going Management Training — Workflow Design — On-Going Advertisement Management

On-Going Dream 100 Marketing — On-Going Lead Tracking — On-Going Online Reputation Management — On-Going Search Engine Optimization — Print Piece Design

 THE PARKE ASSISTED LIVING

**Terry Davis**
Owner / Founder
www.TheParke.net

WILL **YOU** BE THE NEXT SUCCESS STORY?

Schedule your free consultation with Clay Clark today!
www.thrivetimeshow.com

Interested in owning
your own business?

Learn more about
how to open your
very own

# Make Your
# Dog Epic

business location
today at:

**www.MakeYourDogEpic.com**

**PAWS**, for a
Notable Quotable

"Most people are sitting on their own diamond mines. The surest ways to lose your diamond mine are to get bored, become overambitious, or start thinking that the grass is greener on the other side. Find your core focus, stick to it, and devote your time and resources to excelling at it."

**- GINO WICKMAN**

*(The best-selling author of Traction: Get a Grip on Your Business and a guest on Clay Clark's ThrivetimeShow.com Podcast.)*

**PAWS**,
for a Pro Tip

When growing businesses, money is a magnifier. Tyrannical little kings become very tyrannical little kings when you exponentially increase their income.

"Woe to you who plunder, though you have not been plundered; And you who deal treacherously, though they have not dealt treacherously with you! When you cease plundering, You will be plundered; When you make an end of dealing treacherously, They will deal treacherously with you."

**- ISAIAH 33:1**

*(From The Bible)*

"These six things the Lord hates, Yes, seven are an abomination to Him: 17 A proud look, A lying tongue, Hands that shed innocent blood, 18 A heart that devises wicked plans, Feet that are swift in running to evil, 19 A false witness who speaks lies, And one who sows discord among brethren."

**- PROVERBS 6: 16-19**

*(From The Bible)*

"15 Moreover if thy brother shall trespass against thee, go and tell him his fault between thee and him alone: if he shall hear thee, thou hast gained thy brother. 16 But if he will not hear thee, then take with thee one or two more, that in the mouth of two or three witnesses every word may be established. 17 And if he shall neglect to hear them, tell it unto the church: but if he neglect to hear the church, let him be unto thee as an heathen man and a publican."

**- MATTHEW 18:15-17**

*(From The Bible)*

**PAWS**, for a
Notable Quotable

"When one side benefits more than the other, that's a win-lose situation. To the winner it might look like success for a while, but in the long run, it breeds resentment and distrust."

**- DR. STEPHEN R. COVEY**

*(Bestselling author of The 7 Habits of Highly Effective People.)*

**PAWS**, for a
Notable Quotable

"Life is not a dress rehearsal. You must act now because we will all be dead soon and "someday" is not a day that appears on a standard calendar."

**CLAY CLARK**

*(Former Oklahoma Young U.S. SBA Entrepreneur of the Year)*

# ACTION ITEMS

1. Pass on what you've learned by writing a Google Review. search for "ThriveTime Show Jenks" on Google Maps and write a review today!

2. Don't miss a radio show or podcast. Subscribe on Itunes, Spotify, Stitcher or listen at ThrivetimeShow.com

3. Get all of the interactive downloadables by signing up today at ThriveTimeShow.com.

# WANT MORE?

### Check out the Ultimate Textbook for Starting, Running & Growing Your Own Business!

### How to Become Sustainably Rich

NEVER before has entrepreneurship been delivered in an UNFILTERED, real and raw way... until now. This book is NOT for people that want a politically correct and silver-lined happy-go-lucky view of entrepreneurship. That's crap. Supported by case studies and testimonials from entrepreneurs that have grown their businesses all over the planet using these best practice systems, former U.S. Small Business Administration Entrepreneur of the Year, Clay Clark, shares the specific action steps for successful business systems, hilarious stories from situations that every entrepreneur faces, and entrepreneurship factoids that are guaranteed to blow your mind.

# Invite a Friend to Join You at the World's Best 2-Day Intensive Business Workshop

### Get specific and practical training on how to grow your business

# www.ThriveTimeShow.com/Conference

## WANT ONE-ON-ONE MENTORSHIP AND BUSINESS COACHING? VISIT WWW.THRIVETIMESHOW.COM/COACHING

Let our team help you execute your action items and guide you down the proven path (see ThriveTimeShow.com)

"You will never reach your destination if you stop
and throw stones at every dog that barks."

### WINSTON CHURCHILL

*(The Prime Minister of the United Kingdom from 1940 to 1945 who defiantly stood
up alone against Adolf Hitler and the Nazi party's quest to take over the world and to
remove the Jewish people from the planet Earth)*

"Beware of the LITTLE KING for he is weak, fearful, and extremely ineffective."

**CLAY CLARK**